eVolve

Essays on the Virtual Body

C. Jason Smith, Ph.D.

Discipline & Publish Press: Dallas, Texas

Discipline & Publish Press
224 West Campbell Road, Suite 245
Richardson, Texas 75080-3512

C. Jason Smith
eVolve: Essays on the Virtual Body
ISBN: 978-0-359-43918-8
Creative Commons 2.0, 2019
Attribution-Noncommercial-No Derivative Works 2.0 Generic
http://creativecommons.org/licenses/by-nc-nd/2.0/
10 9 8 7 6 5 4 3 2 1

For Luke.

Acknowledgements

I wish to extend my sincerest thanks to several individuals and institutions that helped make this project, which stretched well over fourteen years, possible. My long-time friends and personal critics, Ximena Gallardo C. and Luke Vasilieou, listened to and commented on many stages of this project, whether they knew it or not. Richard Tuerk, author of *OZ in Perspective*, has also continually challenged me and been a dear friend over the years.

I would also like to acknowledge the following colleagues for helping to tame, to a certain extent, a wild mind: Richard Tuerk (Texas A&M University-Commerce), James A. Grimshaw Jr. (TAMU-C), Charles Embry (TAMU-C), Anne Moseley (TAMU-C), Kay Pritchett (The University of Arkansas), Luis Fernando Restrepo (UA), and the late John Locke (UA). Gerald Duchovnay (of TAMU-C and editor of the film journal *Post Script*), Robin Reid (also of TA&MU-C and editor of *The Encyclopedia of Women in Science Fiction*), and Brian Dietrich (Newman University) have been particular professional friends over the years.

The participants and attendees of the Science Fiction and Fantasy Area sessions of the Popular Culture and American Culture Association of the Southwest and Texas listened to numerous presentations on virtuality, gaming, and gender and gave me invaluable feedback. Of that crew I need to single out Alyson Buckman, Tammy Burnett, Brian "Rincewind" Cowlishaw, the indomitable author and the ultimate renaissance-gal Gypsey Teague, the ultimate renaissance-guy Rikk Mulligan, and the inimitable Dean Conrad.

For putting the idea of moving to New York into my head in the first place, I have to blame my long-time friends Geoff Klock and Sara Reiss. The next round is on me.

Conferences in Florida during the New York February freeze are always to be welcomed, and the crew at the International Conference for the Fantastic in the Arts helped tremendously in bolstering my creative spirit and desire to keep writing. Of that boisterous bunch I must acknowledge Sheryl Vint and Mark Bould, editors of *Science Fiction Film and Television*, Joan Gordon, Veronica Hollinger, and Istvan Csicsery-Ronay, Jr. all associated with *Science Fiction Studies*; and former ICFA president and Hugo Award winner Farah Mendelsohn.

I would also like to thank the faculty, staff, and students of LaGuardia Community College of the City University of New York for providing me with a fertile working environment and continual intellectual engagement as well as the Professional Staff Congress of the City University of New York for monetary support for research and writing. I was further very lucky to have the support of the editorial staff of the journal *Reconstruction*, where I have served as Domain Editor for Science, Technology, ad Culture and where an early version of a portion of those works appeared, and particular thanks to Mathew Wolf-Meyer, Davin Heckman, and Alan Clinton for their editorial advice.

I owe a debt for numerous play sessions of *Dungeons & Dragons* and updates on the MMORPG world (and other related shenanigans) to The B.R.A.T.S. of Commerce, Texas (you know who you are), now scattered across Texas, the Southwest, and the rest of the real-life world "out there". Your book is next.

And, finally, as always, to my parents—Janet and Robert "Tubby" Cook and George and Bobbie Smith—who supported me through all with their strength, insights, and love.

Notes on the manuscript

Chapters 2-4 of this work appeared in slightly modified form under the title "Virtual Minds" in the the philosophy journal *Archaepteryx: The Newman Journal of Ideas* (1.1: 2013).

Contents

One: Virtual Lives

In 2001 I came across an article in *Texas Monthly* about an apartment complex in Houston named W@lden that was designed for the high-tech employees of the computer industry.[1] It had, at the time, what was purported to be the fastest domestic internet connection in the world (a T-3) which the residents lovingly called "The Big-Fat Pipe." The main focus of the article was the soap-opera ups and downs, friendships and betrayals, hopes, dreams, and nightmares of this growing class of white-collar geeks living on the tension of the dot-com bubble (and well before the first hints of the burst). Overall, the piece was a localized version of the now infamous stories of The WELL,[2] and countless other online communities like it; but one minor detail of the story of the residents of W@lden stuck with me, and I could not shake the feeling that it said something very important about basic human psychology and how and why we interact with technology.

One of the residents of W@lden told the story of "The Dude". The Dude was a fat young guy who showed up at the apartment complex one day to stay with a friend and proceeded to sit in front of a large computer screen he set up on the floor in the living room and play the massively multiplayer online role-playing game (MMORPG) *EverQuest* for days on end. As days stretched into weeks, he sat in the same spot, moving away from the screen only long enough to answer the door for pizza delivery, grab something to drink, and go to the bathroom. If he slept, which supposedly no one ever saw, he slept in the same spot. Trash piled up around him.

---

[1] Katy Vine, "Love and War in Cyberspace," *Texas Monthly* (Feb. 2001 [29.2]) 80-85, 126-133.

[2] "WELL" is short for Whole Earth 'Lectronic Link. For more about The WELL see, for example, John Seabrook, *Deeper: My Two-Year Odyssey in Cyberspace* (Simon & Schuster , 1997), Katie Hafner's *The WELL: A Story of Love, Death and Real Life in the Seminal Online Community* (Carroll & Graf Publishers , 2001), and Fred Turner, *From Counterculture to Cyberculture: Stewart Brand, the Whole Earth Network, and the Rise of Digital Utopianism* (University of Chicago Press , 2006), to name a few.

I found it difficult not to imagine the detritus of weeks of Pizza Hut deliveries, Big Gulp cups, potato chip bags, and so on. The Dude played *EverQuest* religiously until the so-called friend finally kicked him out and cleaned up the trash, only to find that a dark circular stain had permanently formed in the carpet around the spot where the unwelcome visitor had sat, staring into the flickering light of the computer screen, lost in another world.

Something about that image—the screen, the human body, the virtual world, and the circular stain in the carpet, grabbed hold of my imagination and would not let go. In fact, I thought about it for several years while I co-wrote a book on the *Alien* film series with my partner, Ximena Gallardo C., published several articles on various topics including gender representation in online gaming, and ultimately moved from West Virginia to a new life in New York City. Through it all, there was image of The Dude, now transformed in my mind to "The Dude".

I have been a fan of online games, and specifically MMORPGs, since around 1996 when I started playing an early 3-D online Robotech style game whose exact name I can no longer recall. About that time *Ultima Online*, launched in 1997 by Origin Systems, was hitting the major publications. After reading an article in the 11 March 1999 issue of *Newsweek* about the kid who sold his *Ultima* account for $1500, I charged $9.95 a month to an already over-stressed credit card and gave *Ultima Online* a try. Five minutes of wandering about the virtual town of Delucia and I was hooked on killing (and being killed by) rabbits and chickens and stuffing strange loot in the bank though I had no idea what to do with it all. I played *Ultima Online* for years afterwards and subsequently had my turn at *EverQuest*, and pretty much every other MMORPG that came out. I eventually became a beta-tester (one of the people who play a game for free while in production so the designers can work out problems) on quite a few games. So, certainly, something about the story of The Dude struck home. I too had sat for hours on end at the computer screen lost in the "other world" of light and magic, hacking away at the keys and holding my bladder until the right moment when nothing bad would happen to my online character (just like in real life, there are no "pause" buttons for live games). But my reaction to The Dude seemed broader than mere self-reflection: it seemed somehow more meaningful.

The image I could not get out of my head, the notion that bothered me deeply, was that The Dude was like some sort of religious ascetic engaged in a spiritual quest. I remembered a scene from the Indian epic *The Ramayana* where the hero Rama encounters sages meditating in the forest. They are so deeply in a meditative trance that ants have built swarming hills about their bodies and only their ant-covered heads or faces can be seen. I found that image deeply moving when I read *The Ramayana*. The more I thought about it, and the more I connected The Dude with those shaman, the more intellectually interested I became in my troubling thoughts.

At the time, I considered online gaming—when I thought seriously about it at all—as an extension of table-top role-playing games (RPGs). In the past I had played pencil and paper RPGs such and *Dungeons & Dragons*, participated in the maddeningly slow email version of games at one point, read the "choose your own adventure" books, played solo role-playing video games (RPVGs), and logged-in to early multi-user dimension (MUD) role-playing sites to interact with others in real-time in text-based worlds. *Ultima Online* simply seemed a more visual version of the same thing and the natural progression of the RPG genre. My college buddies and I, now spread out over several states and countries, could log-in at the same time and play together for hours like we used to in college.

When I finally started to think seriously about it, however, I wondered if online RPGs were just a natural progression from the pencil and paper versions, why then did I keep thinking about The Dude? After all, gamers are often obsessive: which is why you will find many current and former gamers in academe. We are an obsessive lot by nature and by training, and it takes a certain amount of intensive focus to conduct research at the required level and sustain it over long periods of time, just as it does to actually master the basic three volumes of *Advanced Dungeons & Dragons* in order to run a game. I suppose all academics are Dungeon Masters in their own way and vice-versa.

My own work at the time that I encountered the story of W@lden and The Dude focused on how notions of gender are expressed and transmitted through technology. My background, however, was in mythology, world literature, and cultural theory; and my graduate training included a heavy dose of psychoanalytic theory and gender criticism, including the usual suspects of Sigmund Freud, Anna Freud, Carl Gustav Jung, and the more recent work of Jacques Lacan and Slovoj Žižek. Of the lot, Jung had a particular attraction for me. I have read his collected works several times, though I was often warned in graduate school that Jung, and his literary descendent Joseph Campbell (author of the best-selling *The Hero with a Thousand Faces*) were "out of favor" in academic circles, and that my time working towards publications would be better spent elsewhere.

Obediently, I turned to the French philosopher Michele Foucault and the American gender theorist Judith Butler and found myself happily working with sex and gender construction in literature and film. But, I did not give up my affinity with Jung's work and something about the story of The Dude seemed distinctly Jungian. I could use other words, of course, such as "mythic," "epic," "religious," or any other number of terms to indicate a sense of transcendence, of something bigger than ourselves, but the sense is the same. The Dude was not simply playing *EverQuest* (albeit obsessively), he was, like the ascetics and mystics, travelling to a magical Somewhere Else and leaving his mortal flesh behind.

And there we come to the point: where the residents of the apartment complex saw The Dude as an obsessive, out of control, weirdo, loser (a shocking mirror of themselves in many aspects, as the author of the article indicates), I began to see him as the contemporary embodiment of the ancient archetypal story of a certain type of religious figure. Fat, slovenly, unwashed, and reeking, The Dude was having what amounts to a religious experience. He was travelling in other plains of existence, virtually

4

disembodied in his rejection of all but the most essential needs of physical survival.

He wasn't exactly living on bread and water, of course, but the general principle was the same. What was distinctly different from his religious predecessors, however, was the means of transcendence. Rather than mantras or koans, the *Analects* of Confucius, or the *Tao Te Ching* of Lao Tzu; rather than the stories of Rama or Krishna or the Buddha, or the poetry of the "Song of Songs" from the Torah and Old Testament, The Dude had *EverQuest*: a computer mediated virtual environment, more specifically termed a persistent state world (PSW), massively multi-player online role-playing game (again MMORPG, which is intriguingly pronounced "morgue").

This was several years before a young South Korean man, Seungseob Lee, died after playing *StarCraft* for 50 hours straight in an internet café in 2005, and not long before the short film "The Kid" from *The Animatrix* (released in 2003) implied suicide can set you free from the world we know to the "real world" outside "The Matrix". William Gibson, of course, set the tone for this level of immersion in his inimitable *Neuromancer* (1984) where we see two variations on the same theme: the immersive entertainment console and the hacker lost in cyberspace who leaves his "meat body" behind. But what Gibson saw and what he described in the video arcade that served as the basis for his idea of cyberspace was for him *something new* and potentially, for all of us, *horrifying*. When I read *Neuromancer* as a teenager, I had the same feeling: we were in the process of something new, a "terrible beauty," as Yeats might have described it. Though admittedly it was sometimes difficult to see the future Gibson described in a game of *Space Invaders* (Midway, 1978), *Centipede* (Atari 1981), or *Ms. Pac Man* (Midway, 1982), I can still fell the immersion of the first-person perspective of the early flight game *Red Baron* (Atari, 1980).[3]

---

[3] See, for example, "Red Baron (1980 video game)" on Wikipedia: http://en.wikipedia.org/wiki/Red_Baron_(1980_video_game).

After reading the story of The Dude, however, I suddenly had the opposite sense: I was not seeing something new, but seeing something deeply psychological and monstrously ancient, what Jung would have called "archetypal," perhaps; and it was on those terms that it interested me. At the time I had trouble putting a name to it. Was what I was seeing in The Dude a symbol or symbolic action? Was it a story being enacted? Was it the horror of the unruly, filthy body and the stain it left behind? Or was it, on the other hand, the pristine virtual landscapes and the sleek virtual bodies that occupied it: bodies of light that do not sweat, defecate, or urinate? In fact, I had no idea what the "something" I was feeling was nor what it meant. Finally, I decided that the question I was really asking was "What are the pieces of the puzzle, the strands of influence and confluence, that made up this *act* embodied by The Dude?"

Most obviously we have a human body interacting with a technology—a moment in time—so I started there, with The Dude and worked my way back along the path of bodies and technologies that led up to the moment represented by The Dude. It was not a straight path. If you can imagine looking at one bud on one tiny twig on one branch of an enormous ancient oak tree, and then tracing back down to the root, that would be analogous to the perception that opened up for me as I worked my way back through the innumerable technologies and psychological structures that added up to that one moment, of that one body, sitting before that one screen, and interacting with thousands of other bodies sitting in front of thousands of computer screens. I set out purposefully to track the origin of the moment and, as a writer, to write about it if I could.

I realized that I needed to get a handle on the language, the terminology, of my investigation, and the first term that needed to be addressed was "virtual reality." Having been formally trained in English, Spanish, and Arabic, I knew my way around a dictionary and own a couple of dozen myself, but in this case, I planned to hit the Oxford English Dictionary—first the multi-volume print version then, later, online (they both have distinct advantages)—to find the origins of the term. I knew that origins can tell us a lot about the hidden meanings of a word or phrase and what they mean historically. But first, I sat down and wrote out what I thought "virtual reality" meant so that I would have a record of my perceptions before they were changed by the formal definitions (the denotations), cultural references (or connotation), and history of the word (the etymology).

What I knew was that virtual reality (VR for short hereafter) was hot in popular culture and promised to remain so for quite some time. Films such as *Total Recall* (1990), *The Lawnmower Man* (1992), and later *The Matrix* film series, and *Eternal Sunshine of the Spotless Mind* (2004), to name a few, draw on the enduring popularity of computer games which has elevated a technical computer concept to the level of cultural phenomenon. Even more, these films seemed to be rooted in serious philosophical issues that invoked potential long-lasting cultural implications. The most popular of these films *The Matrix, The Matrix: Reloaded* and *The Matrix: Revolutions* (1999, 2003, and 2003 respectively) each explores the age-old fear of technology replacing humans in the world's hierarchy and invokes the very essence of philosophy by asking "What is real?"

In the popular media, parents and politicians obsess about violence in video games. Around the world millions of people log into virtual environments to interact with people they have never met in real life (or RL in the lingo) and more and more often these interactions involve virtual bodies (called "avatars") inhabiting virtual spaces. Games like *The Sims Online* (now defunct), *EverQuest, World of Warcraft*, and the first really popular of these massively multiplayer online role-playing games, the iconic *Ultima Online*, take video games to a new level that moves beyond simple one on one action into a fully designed world where hundreds and even thousands of players can engage together in long drawn out narratives in worlds that never (or *almost* never) "turn off." Like real-life (RL), this VR continues with or without you.

Virtual Reality—the very mention of the term invokes images of computer-generated fantasy worlds. The general denotation of the term from a standard dictionary, however, turned out to be quite mundane: a construction that expresses or manifests the virtues of human experience. But what did the Oxford English Dictionary have to say about it? I decided to first have a go at the 20-volume library print edition that contains the etymology (or history) of virtually every word in the English language. Though obviously the online version is more up to date, I felt that looking for my terms in the more traditional format would give me some grounding in traditional research before I hit the web. When I began reading the entry, I was actually quite surprised at how much information there was on "virtual reality". The phrase "virtual reality" was first used in computer science to describe a computer-generated environment in the late 1980's by computer scientist Jaron Lanier, who claims to have coined the term. However, the origin of the term is actually a bit more convoluted. For example, the pioneering computer artist Myron Krueger coined the term "artificial reality" in the 1970's; the French poet, playwright, and actor Antonin Artaud used the term "*la réalite virtuelle*" in his 1938 book *The Theater and Its Double*; and science fiction author Damien Broderick used the term "virtual reality" in a related sense in his 1982 novel *The Judas Mandala*. But it was Lanier who invested himself in the term and popularized it.

It certainly felt to me like it had been around much longer than that, but then I remembered that William Gibson used the conflated term "cyberspace" and not "virtual reality." But we should remember that even scientists and engineers tend to choose terms for the potential "buzz" they might start. Like the coining of the term "Chaos Theory" for popular descriptions of the theories arising from the field of "complex dynamics" caused great furor due to its philosophical and religious connotations, "virtual reality" is a term composed of not one historically loaded term, or even two, but three interrelated terms. "Virtual Reality" is based on the complex philosophical concepts of "virtual," and "reality," obviously, but also "virtue" (the root of "virtual") which is a close conceptual corollary to "reality." In fact, "virtual" is an adjective that already implies a "reality" being emulated, therefore saying "virtual reality" is rather like saying, as second-rate Tex-Mex restaurants are wont to do, *"chili con queso* with cheese." Of the long and complicated history of the three interrelated terms, I would like to draw attention to several factors which will have a direct impact on this history of the idea.

First, the word "virtue," the noun form of "virtual," is strongly associated through much of the development of the English language with the power or powers of the divine; thus, to "have virtue" was to exhibit or embody some quality of the divine power. The important point here is that to "have virtue" meant to *embody* the divine, to open oneself up to an external power and let it in. Thus, Jesus embodied all virtues because he was God embodied— what may be called an "avatar" from the Sanskrit *"avatara"*: a term that will have relevance to our later discussion. Likewise, the hero and heroine of the *Ramayana*, Rama and Sita, and have both been described as avatars of the Hindu god Vishnu (the 7th and 8th, respectively). But, we will come back to avatars later.

Second, the word "virtue" is historically tied to gender. "Virtue" is from the Latin *virtus* meaning "excellence, potency, efficacy" but more literally "manliness," the root *vir* indicating "man" as in "human and male." Thus, virtue is a quality, power, or essence that has its roots in the male body and is, therefore, no doubt tied to the most obvious symbol of male power, the phallus, as both the male sexual organ and the symbol of masculine strength. For if "vir" indicates the male then it must originally refer to that obvious indicator of sex from birth.

Through time, the virtues expanded in scope and divided into "active" and "passive" virtues. Predictably, those qualities not considered "masculine," albeit still associated with the divine, came to be associated with women. These "civilizing virtues" of faith, hope, and charity, and so on, contrasted and complimented the more masculine virtues such as justice and the all-encompassing honor. These virtues were also associated with women in form if not in actuality. Justice, like Liberty, is portrayed most often as a woman, and women become "the keeper" of male honor, and thereby the family honor as well, though they do not "defend it" or "wield it." Therefore, the term "virtual," tied up as it is in the complex web of signification surrounding "virtue," is a term heavily imbued through time with gender issues and gendered meanings.

Third, "the virtual" is part and parcel of an ancient philosophical and theological discourses on representation, imitation, and simulation, including Plato and Aristotle's classical discourses on *mimesis*, the Buddha's meditations on the nature of lived reality as illusion, the Christian notion of Heaven (all from around 500 B.C.), and in contemporary discourse, Jean Baudrillard's critique of simulacra in *Simulacra and Simulation*. The term, therefore, invokes a long history of discourse on the nature or reality: what the philosophers call "ontology."

In general, then, the "virtual" is something that has the qualities of something else without actually, or literally, being that thing. However, just to confuse matters further, it could effectively be that thing at which point the line between the "real" and the "simulacrum" would blur. A woman named "Faith" for example could also embody the virtue of her name and, therefore, "be Faith [by name]" and "have faith" and "act out of faith" where the inscribing of the name to the child was in hope of enacting that virtue within her body and life. This was, perhaps, more true in an earlier era but we still understand this naming business when we name our children. Few people would want to name their children names such like "Satan," "Adolf," or even "Loser" as we would fear the social repercussions as well as the possibility of invoking the traits of the namesake.

What we term "the virtual" is, in philosopher Jean Baudrillard's terms, a "simulacrum"—the virtual simulates something else that approaches reality, though it never quite attains it. Though we have given the term "virtual" a new shine with computer technology, the concept itself (and even the word in one form or another) is very, very old; and I believe, and will attempt to demonstrate, that is cuts to the core of what it means to be human. By my way of thinking, to be human is to be self-reflexive, to wonder about ourselves, our origins, our place in the universe, our destiny. Thus, "virtue," and its adjectival form "virtual," are core concepts of the human experience.

10

Our fourth concern is that the term "reality" is one of those terms like "god" and "virginity" that everyone assumes they understand when they do not and assumes everyone else knows when they cannot. We are all supposedly somehow in silent agreement. If we start to talk about it, however, we quickly recognize that while everyone seems to "know" it, no one seems to agree what "it" is. For example, I teach a course on sexuality in literature and every single semester I ask my student-learners to raise their hands if they know what a "virgin" is. They all seem to. I then ask each student the following: "Please write a definition of 'virgin,' limiting it only to the human female to avoid confusion." They think. They write. They all smile happily when done, comfortable in the knowledge that they all have "the right answer." (It is, after all, very early in the semester yet). "So," I ask, "what is a 'virgin'?" "A person who has not had sex!" exclaims one young woman. "Everyone agree? OK, then, all we have to do is define 'sex' and we'll be done and can move on to the poetry for the day! So, what is sex?"

Imagine a well-trained choir all secretly handed a different song, singing the first note in what they assume will be unison only to produce an ear-splitting cacophony of disagreement followed by nervous confusion. Is it "penis and vagina"? "Intercourse"? "Breaking of the hymen"? "Oral sex"? "Any sexual contact"? What is "sexual contact"? Do you have to "fall in love to really lose your virginity"? I have heard all of these and the tendency to over-share is strong in this situation—one young woman claimed to be a virgin because she's never been "on bottom." Another student a few years ago asserted in all seriousness to the class that, even though she had given birth to a child, she was still a virgin. I thought it improper at that juncture to pursue that particular line of reasoning any further, but I think the point has been made. The is no general popular agreement on what exactly, constitutes the sex act that removes virginity.

You might be surprised at the sheer number of responses to what seems like a simple question, and a question that seems so fundamental to the sexual mores of a society. They invariably laugh and call each other "liars" and "idiots" in an attempt to force the individual's reality onto the collective whole. Rather than admit the subjective (and political) nature of an apparently essential term like "virginity" or "sex," each of my students would rather suppress all of those "other" voices. But, by the end of the class, the point is clear—"virginity" is not only a natural state, but a socially constructed and culturally invested phenomenon used to define and, thereby control, bodies through cultural created mores and laws.

"Reality" may not be quite as contentious as the nature of virginity, but it operates much to the same effect. As far as the dictionary definition, or denotation, goes, "reality" is historically tied to "property" or "land" (therefore "*real*-estate," or actual property, as opposed to money or investments) and the root of "real" specifically refers to the fixed nature of land or property— that which is immovable and unchangeable. As they say in my home state of Texas, "Land is the only thing that is real."

The "real" refers directly to a particular *virtue* of things which makes them exactly what they seem or purport to be, so that "a real wrestler" embodies the traits of the wrestler in a way which posits the person as defining the term itself (a measure by which to test other wrestler's skill) while at the same time acknowledging that simulation is possible and denying the simulation in this particular manifestation: if Joe is a "real wrestler" then others who purport to be "real wrestlers" must really be just playing the part (pretenders or mere simulations). To say something is "real," therefore, is to admit the possibility of mistaking it for the simulation (a simulacrum) as when an advertisement on a juice carton reads "real juice" or as I ran into recently while shopping for milk, "real milk from real cows"—a phrase designed to call into question the "reality" of the other brands of milk on the shelf.

In common speech there are three major schools of thought on reality that have been succinctly summarized in baseball metaphor as the three different varieties of baseball umpires. Reality 1: "Some are balls, and some are strikes, and I call them *as they are.*" Reality 2: "Some are balls, and some are strikes, and I call them *as I see them.*" Reality 3: "Some are balls, and some are strikes, but *they ain't nothing until I call them*". The first group—"Hey! A strike is a strike!"—espouses the objective view of reality which essentially argues that reality exists, and reasonable humans have access to that reality through observation and the application of formal logic. Anyone who does not agree has not properly applied their observation and logic to the event. Most scientists would fall into this category, though certainly not all (some of the quantum mechanics physicists among them).

The second group—"I'm a trained umpire doing the best I can under the circumstances"—believes that reality is a bit more difficult to get at primarily due to the slippery nature of language, in this case the "rules" of the game, and our inability to describe what we perceive to others. This ambiguity is compounded with our cultural prejudices to "see" what we have been taught to see or, worse, want to see. Thus, an umpire born and raised and trained in Texas might be accused of favoritism when calling balls in Queens, particularly if the Rangers are playing. If he also ascribes to this view of reality, he knows he could be prejudiced but does his best to exceed his upbringing and follow his training.

The final category of umpire knows that he is the first and last authority on balls and strikes (at least in this game) and that is because the rules of the game give him the power to decide reality within the context of the game: "What I say goes!" And because the rules of the game and the authority are behind him, the record books will thereafter record a strike regardless of those yahoos who (operating in Reality 2) argue about it for years. This view holds that authority, derived from law or other source of power, sets the nature of reality. Umpires collectively define what a strike is or is not in general, and specific umpires decide in every specific case, and each umpire has the power, as defined by rule, to decide what *is* or *is not* a strike in the reality of that game. This view of reality we might term *observer dependent* (from physics) or *informatics* (the science of information): essentially we might say that those who control the rules (information) define what the rest of us—including the players and the fans—experience as reality.

Since receiving my Ph.D. some years ago, my father takes great pleasure in annoying me with the old question "If a tree falls in the woods and there is no one there to hear it, does it make a sound?" The range of answers includes "Yes, of course," "No, because 'sound' is a function of 'hearing'," and "How would I know if I wasn't there?" to "How do you know it fell if you weren't there?" My favorite answer for him, though I change it up to keep him entertained, is "Well, it depends on whether it is a real tree and a real sound or a hypothetical tree and a hypothetical sound." I tend to be a bit of a smart-ass with my father. Regardless, though the above is an extreme oversimplification of the variety and depth of ontology, it should suffice for the moment for our inquiry into the nature of "virtual reality" to proceed.

Let us finish, then with the assertion that "virtual reality" means literally "something that exhibits the virtues of reality to some degree." Thus, a virtual room would have a doorway and walls and a floor and a ceiling and any of the other "virtues" that imply a room. What makes this room a "virtual room" as opposed to a "real room"? The one trait that the real room has that the virtual does not is that the real room does not require a technical mediator in order for a person with the usual range of senses to experience it, whereas the virtual room requires that the senses of my body be in some way augmented or modified for the duration of the experience. I go into a room, but the virtual room has to come to me by fooling my senses in some way.

For example, we have early examples of virtual art in rooms that were painted to simulate forests. The paint and painter's technique is a technology that interacts with the senses in an attempt to fool them. Burning pine incense in the room would further the illusion as would covering the floor with pine-needles and so on. The virtual room may seem, then, more "interactive" than a plain room because of our awareness of its artificiality and our desire to interact with it and "test it out," so to speak, by touching the walls and looking for the source of the pine smell. We wonder at the illusion of the created "virtual reality" and enjoy it but this also may lead to our questioning the nature of "reality" as well. After all, why else would we enjoy a room of fake trees if it did not make us see real trees in new ways. Perhaps more trouble is the idea that if we can see the real in new ways then how "real" is it? Which is to say, for good or ill the virtual pushes us towards Reality 3: "they ain't nothing until I call them" while at the same time hiding the means of production of the simulation: we do not see the process of the painting of the trees on the wall. This concept is just one step away from games like *World of Warcraft*. Virtual spaces are created for the players who have no access to the means of their creation (the rules and coding that are the real game).

All of which led me to some very interesting and uncomfortable ideas on which to base my investigation. I started to think that the notion of "virtual reality" is based upon three central concerns of the human experience. First, it depends on the experience or belief that the human body is a "made" thing. This is not a particularly novel idea. After all, most mythology systems include a creation story where humans are created from mud or ash or ribs or some such. Humans are embodied beings; therefore, part of the "illusion" of this world is that very embodiment. No wonder we imagine a part of the body that is eternal, can escape and travel around without the body, can go to heaven, or can be born again. Like virtue, the notion of a soul or spirit, of an eternal part that survives our death is so prevalent that "virtue" and "soul" seem to operate as mutually supporting metaphors. As we shall see, however, virtue arises from the primal body and gives birth to such notions as the soul and eternity.

Second, reality—our experience in the world—seems to many of us to be not only subjective (meaning prone to distortion by the individual senses and mind) but also very limited. Throughout recorded history humans have been convinced that there was more to the universe than meets the eye and that "reality" was not the whole story. As Calderon de la Barca wrote more than 300 years ago, "*La vida es sueno*" ["Life is a dream"]. Life is a dream of our own making—or even more terrifying, life is a dream made for us by others as in Plato's "Allegory of the Cave". This is the fear expressed in a broad range of literary works: even those written for children. For example, in Lewis Carroll's *Alice in Wonderland* Tweedle Dee suggests to Alice that "If that there King [who dreams the world into existence] was to wake, you'd go out 'Bang!' just like a candle!"

For Plato in classical Greece, Buddha in India, and Jesus in the Middle East, and many others who believed variations on the theme that the "world is a dream," all the common man calls "reality," what we experience through our senses every single day, *is* virtual, exhibiting the qualities (the virtues) of reality but hiding the *real reality* behind it (heaven, nirvana, the Real). This notion is the basis for all religion and theology and much philosophy. Our inescapably human feeling that *this can't be all there is* leads us to the belief that all *this* is somehow not *real* and is therefore a copy of what is real that has somehow been lost. Thus, we come to the postmodern pop-psych mantra that "I just don't feel like myself anymore."

Freudian psychoanalytic theorist Jacques Lacan describes this sense of loss as the very basis for the establishment of the ego. In effect it is the pain of losing the Real (or uninhibited participation with the world) that makes us individuated persons. Or at least makes us believe we are individuated persons. And what causes this primary trauma? Language. Once I say "I" there has to be a "you" and we are lonely and misunderstood ever after, trapped in a world that is not quite as it should be, not quite *real*, trapped as it were in a virtual world. And, according to Lacan, thank heaven for orgasms because that is the closest you'll ever get again to feeling "at one with the universe" again.

Orgasms aside, I believe now, at the end of the long journey that culminated in this book, that the virtual is our Alpha and Omega, our beginning and end, and that it ties together the great web of what we call "being human". So, let's start at the beginning, at the root of the tree, and see how far up the branches we can go. To do that, however, we will need some sense of the layout of the branches of knowledge that we will be delving into. Starting from an online game like *EverQuest* or *World of Warcraft* what groups of technologies or techniques are necessary for the event of engaging in that online space to happen at all?

Working from the image of the virtual environment on the computer screen I can begin my list by saying the existence of that moment requires the ability to represent bodies and to recognize those representations (or what we might call representational art or technology). I can see a body on the screen, what is called my "avatar" for reasons we will get into later. It was designed by an artist and I can recognize it for what it is supposed to be (a body) and what it actually is (a simulated body). That body occupies a space in the screen, and that space too was created, and I can recognize this created, virtual space as being like the space I occupy. For those spaces to be created and for me to understand them (to see what they are or are supposed to be) requires a basic understanding of geography (negotiating spaces) and cartography (visualizing spaces) and cartography also requires an understanding of artificially rendered perspective (imagining spaces from positions other than standing in them).

To understand the unfolding of the online game, I must have some grasp of narrative structures to be able to follow the "story" (the story of my character and/or the unfolding story of the virtual world as a whole) from point to point, and that story has to be conveyed to me. This technique is based in our human ability to tell stories, to make narratives, and transmit stories through time and space as in mythology and history. Narratives themselves include the ability to imagine bodies moving through space and time as we have to "imagine" the events of the story as we hear them. Though I do not need to be aware of it to play an online game, the online environment requires the additional understanding of the actual rules of movement in spaces through time and the ability to formulate new rules of bodies and spaces and times (logistics) as movement in simulated environments is based on our movement but is not the same. Movement is, however, based on rules, which is part of what makes it a "game."

But what is a "game"? We might think of the difference between throwing dirt in the air (play), to stacking blocks in a pattern (an individual game), to a game with more formal rules such as Hide and Seek, or even more complex, *Dungeons and Dragons*. *EverQuest* is certainly more complex than hide and seek, but the same basic principles are there. Speaking of *Dungeons & Dragons*, our MMO is also a Role-Playing Game (or RPG), making it an MMORPG and all RPG's are based in *Dungeons & Dragons* (actually its predecessor *Chainmail*) which are in turn rooted in the rules (logistics again) of miniature war gaming.

And then, of course, we have the computer itself. For all of the above to happen, the PC must bring together a long history of technologies that include the ability to record and transmit sound and/or data, record and transmit images, record and transmit moving images, produce computing power, design and encode computer games, design and encode computer text-based role-playing games, design and encode video games then multi-player video games, connect computers together into a network to form the Internet, and then combine elements to produce multiplayer internet text-based environments followed by the addition of video-game technology to produce massively multi-player online role-playing games like *World of Warcraft*. That is a lot of technologies and techniques.

Stripping out all of the potential sub-categories for the moment a short list of the broad clusters of technologies and techniques needed for me to log in to an online game like *World of Warcraft* might break down into a list like this:

- Representation of bodies (representational art)
- Representation of spaces (cartography and representational art)
- Telling stories or creating and conveying narratives of events (narrative)
- Describing how bodies move in space and time (logistics)
- Inventing rules that simulate reality (role-play and formal games)
- Information recording technologies (such as writing, music records, DVD's, or hard-drives)
- Information transmission and reception technologies (such as books, radio, television, the Internet, and WiFi)
- Computing power (mainframes and personal computers)

This list is, of course, only one way to think of some of the different technologies that support a virtual environment, and any list is, by its very nature, exclusive. However, what I like about this list as a starting point is that it clearly demonstrates the process of producing virtual environments as a historically rooted progression and compiling of technologies and techniques. The representation of bodies, for example, historically precedes the representation of space, which necessarily must come before narrative as "stories" involve bodies moving in space and time (for example, "He went to the store.") which in turn precedes the invention of rules that simulate bodies moving in space and time (such as in a chess game where the figures represent individuals or armies and the board a country or collection of countries). Still, we have an imposing list to say the least, but if we want to come to some sort of understanding of the story of The Dude, then I will need to start somewhere on that list. One of my professors, James A. Grimshaw Jr., was fond of asking students a question about tackling a large research project. "How do you eat and elephant?" he would ask, one eyebrow rising slightly up his pale forehead. We would all wait for the answer in mute silence, though many of us had been in his classes before and already knew the answer. He would smile slightly, lean in to the class confidentially, "How do you eat an elephant?" he would ask again, and deliver his line: "One bite at a time, people. One . . . bite . . . at . . . a . . . . time."

Taking that to heart, then, I will begin at what seems to be the first bite: the emergence of representational art and the simulation of bodies.

Two: Making Bodies

In the late 1990's, the sexy female video game hero Lady Lara Croft was kicking-ass across the pages of American magazines and fighting her way into the hearts of game players worldwide. Across the globe millions of teen boys (and some girls) were playing a female action adventure hero in Tomb Raider. With her impossible body and. equally impossible acrobatics, Lara Croft sashayed her way into the hearts of millions players of all ages.

Lady Laura Croft, an Indiana Jones style archeologist from a British noble family, fought them all with her ubiquitous twin pistols and sometimes—if the player was skilled enough or lucky enough—she triumphed. More often Lara died. As was the case with my own feeble attempts at the game, she died, and she died, and she died some more. She fell off cliffs onto spikes, drowned, smashed into walls, was bludgeoned to death by falling traps and generally had a miserably bloody time of it all around, but she always came back as good as new, ready to swing her long braid towards adventure and imminent death once again.

Lara Croft from *Tomb Raider*

Now a popular film series starring Angelina Jolie as Lady Croft, the sheer popularity of the franchise was both overwhelming and unexpected. It may seem normal now for both men and women to play games with protagonists of varying genders, or even no gender at all, but at the time of its release Lara Croft was really something new. For several years I read magazine articles, and listened to myriad academic papers, about exploring the perils of this latest expression of violence towards women, Lara Croft as an expression of female power, Lara Croft as a role model for young women, Lara Croft as the expression of rampant imperialism, Lara Croft as the expression of post-colonial angst, the psychological benefits of cross-gender identification, the psychological risks of cross-gender identification, and on and on.

What I found fascinating as I sat reading the newest article or listening to the latest neo-Marxist reading of Lady Croft's adventures was that so many people from so many different walks of life were playing and writing about a video game. A video game? Seriously?

As I listened to bright-eyed graduate students justify the hours and hours spent playing *Tomb Raider* instead of studying for comprehensives or working on theses and dissertations by applying whatever critical approach was at hand or hot at the moment (at that time Michel Foucault and Judith Butler) I began to see that all this theorizing was a well-researched smokescreen subconsciously constructed and executed by the critic-fan community to hide one fact: Lara Croft was not real. Yes, she was beautiful and sexy, and we enjoyed playing her and guiding her to her win and lose and live and die, but what really mattered was that Lara was a created woman who was intentionally designed to "turn us on" on many different psychological levels including her virtual death. There is something deeply imbedded in us that responds to the artifice of the female form and the destruction of that form *(eros* and *thanatos)*.

Even more: making representations of the human form, and particularly the female form, is one of the oldest art forms we know, and some argue it is *the oldest*. Thus, body representation serves as the first evidence for, and perhaps the jumping off point or "alpha incident," for everything we now consider "human culture". Any art history book will tell you that the oldest pieces of representational art, those that depict bodies, were generally called the "Venus figurines". Though, being more than 35,000 years old, they are obviously not part of the myth of the Greco-Roman goddess Aphrodite/Venus, the assumption was that these figurines were the earliest ancestors of statues like the famous Venus de Milo. We have some indications of decorative arts previous to these figures, but the symmetrical scratchings on the surfaces of simple bone tools are not representational in the sense that they do not try to represent physical forms but, rather, patterns that may have been the product of the attempt to reproduce the patters of visual illusions such as those caused by staring into the sun or the result of early trance states.[4] To understand how this might come about, all you have to do is look at a smooth surface such as a piece of blank paper, then look into a bright light for a few moments, then look back at the paper and new shapes will magically appear. Try to trace those shapes on the paper while you still "see" them and you have pretty much discovered the "meaning" behind the earliest human attempts at representation.

The Woman of Willendorf, c. 24000 BCE.

---

[4] See, for example, David Lewis-Williams' *The Mind in the Cave: Consciousness and the Origins of Art* (London: Thames & Hudson, 2004).

The most famous of the bunch of small figurines is the so-called Woman of Willendorf (or "Venus of Willendorf"). I first learned about this figurine in a class on sex and gender taught by Dr. Lisa Stark, then at what is now Texas A&M University-Commerce (formerly East Texas State University). Dr. Stark was a spunky, newly minted Ph.D. with research interests in sex and gender, Shakespeare, the silent film star Louise Brooks (who she bore more than a passing resemblance to), and the pop-singer Madonna. In her class we covered the gamut of sex and gender theory in art, history, psychology, literature (the supposed subject of the class), television, film, and print media, including a healthy dose of pornography. It was a truly exciting course that felt, somehow, *dangerous*. After all, who knew our library carried subscriptions to both *Playboy* and *Penthouse* at the request of the Psychology Department? As graduate students at a rural university that had traditionally been a teacher's college (what had been called in an earlier era a "normal college" which I still find amusing) we were thrilled by the contemporary piratical feel to the class, and I developed an obsession with psychology and critical theory that obviously continues unabated.

We started the class with a slide and video presentation that began with the Woman of Willendorf and ran through, as I recall, a visual history of the female body in art culminating with Madonna performing as Marilyn Monroe in "Material Girl" and as a private dancer in "Open Your Heart". Having been a Political Science undergraduate with very little exposure to the then burgeoning field of Cultural Studies, it took years before many of the ideas presented in the class began to sink in and make sense. I still find new ideas and discover new meanings in all the texts we read and interacted with in the class, and the Woman of Willendorf was no exception. Therefore, it seems entirely appropriate to return to her now in this discussion of virtual culture.

The Woman of Willendorf (unearthed in 1908 near Willendorf, Austria) is a little sculpture with a length of 11.1 centimeters (or 4 ¼ inches) which fits snugly in the palm of the hand. The simplest way to describe the Woman of Willendorf is that she (for it is clearly a female) is all breasts, belly, buttocks, and vagina. There is a head without a face—she is either wearing a woven mask or looking down and showing only her plaited hair—diminutive arms, and plump thighs leading to footless calves, but little else. Though she was originally dubbed the "Venus of Willendorf" because of a visual similarity in the minds of the archeologists to the Venus de Milo and the early presumption that the figurine represented a fertility goddess, there is some disagreement as to whether she is merely corpulent, a fat body being a symbol of wealth and prosperity to hunters and gatherers, or pregnant, making her more likely to be a fertility symbol.

My impressions were, and still are, that the enlarged vaginal area and large breasts as well as the vestigial arms resting protectively on the breasts would seem to indicate pregnancy and an impending birth, while the buttocks and thighs look simply fat as from a diet made up of large amounts of fatty foods. Therefore, I have no problem seeing her as both a symbol of wealth and prosperity and female fecundity. But, that is just me using what I know about gender and culture to make an intelligent guess. What she meant to her creator and to her viewers—what her purpose was in their culture—is another matter altogether. What we do know is that more than 12,000 years before man was painting animals on cave walls he was walking the ancient plains with sex in his hand.

It is odd considering the size that most photographs of the figurine make it look enormous. No doubt this occurs through a desire to show the details of the work. The effect, however, is to give the figurine a sense of massive historical importance in direct opposition to its physical size, and I have come to think that these images are telling: whatever she might have represented then, she is now our Eve. She is the first "woman" made by or out of "man" by which I mean this is the first indication we have that humans had become conscious of the fact that "woman" was a different thing from "man," conscious enough to be self-conscious about it and carve a figure representing that difference. We really don't need to know what it was *used for* after it was made, the fact that it exists at all tells us what we need to know: the sexed body had come into existence as something to think about. Humans were no longer just "having sex" as all animals do, they had begun to *make sex*. This little stubby piece of rock may seem a far cry from Lara Croft, but the essential elements are all there—both Lara and the Woman of Willendorf are *made girls*: fantasies from an individual human mind made manifest for all to see.

In his groundbreaking work *The Mind in the Cave* (2004), Anthropologist David Lewis-Williams convincingly argues that early art, and in particular cave drawings, are not simply crude artistic representation of "a day in the life" of early humans. Rather, examples of cave art, such as the famous images of Lascaux, are the result of dream states (self-induced or otherwise) where the artist was essentially "seeing" the images in the shapes of the rock and believed they were looking "through" the rock into another world. What they drew, according to Lewis-Williams, was an attempt to release from the stone the beings on the "other side," as it were, in the spirit realm.

After reading *The Mind in the Cave*, I imagined our figurine artist using a rib-bone tool to carve the figure, to set his little Eve free, to release her from the rock so she could bring her magic of birth and rebirth, of the change of seasons and the phases of the moon into the world. Though the rib-bone tool is a complete fantasy based on my own desire to make some poetic reference to the Book of Genesis, Lewis-Williams' notion of seeing figures in surfaces and trying to release them rings true in the case of the Woman of Willendorf. I think the artist saw the woman in the rock—saw his own desire for a woman and all she represents including sex, offspring, bountiful food, a warm partner at night, her cycles and the associated magic of the cycles of the seasons and the moon, and etc.—and set about to free her from the rock so she could be his and he could share in that magic.

This is what C. G. Jung meant by the archetype he termed the "Anima": the idea of Woman with a capital "W" as viewed through the male psyche. But while archetypes may have universal characteristics across human cultures they are not static; rather, they are dynamic. Which mean that they move forward through time and, doing so, they proliferate and change, but the root still remains. From the Woman of Willendorf we may trace forward a history of sex and gender culminating in our own manifestations of the Anima in supermodels and Hollywood stars. The Woman of Willendorf is, as it were, a virtual "woman"—or the first "woman"—representing the properties of "woman" as understood by an individual within a defined cultural framework. She is the first notion, the first expression, the first definition of "woman."

We see in the Woman of Willendorf the act of making bodies, making images of bodies, and thereby imagining sex and bringing it into being as a cultural trope (or idea) as an essential human activity in the most basic way. And the mind that made the Woman of Willendorf is essentially that same mind that designs avatars for *EverQuest* and *World of Warcraft*. Which is why, though separated by millennia, we can immediately recognize the Woman of Willendorf as human and understand that it is a human female.

Once our ancestors began to see three dimensional shapes in rocks such as the bodies of people and animals, it was a short step to seeing three dimensional images in increasingly "flat" surfaces such as rock faces and cave walls. The rock faces operated as a concealing screen between this world and the other realm of spirit. For the cave artist, according to Lewis-Williams, the paintings had a three-dimensional quality as they reached into that "other world," and at least some of the images incorporate features of the surface of the rock into the image, further indicating the three-dimensional quality of the works. But we were well on our way to being able to understand two dimensional images as simulations of three-dimensional space. It is not that far at all from the Woman of Willendorf, the cave walls of Lascaux, and the screen of my Alienware computer. Once we could imagine bodies and manifest them for view, it was perhaps inevitable to begin representing spaces for those bodies to occupy.

Three: Making Space

I am an explorer. Or, at least I am a *virtual* explorer. The minute I log-in to a new, online virtual environment such as *Second Life* or *World of Warcraft* the first thing I want to do is try to run through walls, fall off cliffs, and reach the edge of the fantasy world. I may stop to fight an orc, an alien, or a killer rabbit here and there, but that is just a pit-stop on the road to see everything and go everywhere possible. If I can do all that without dying, the more the better; but in all honesty, I die a lot. Which is to say my virtual characters die a lot--and that probably explains why I am a virtual explorer but a real world professor. There's a lot less dying in the professor business, and I am rather fond of breathing and eating and drinking red wine. Movies are nice too, but they don't come up until a later chapter. What I want to discuss now is that joy of discovery that fuels exploration and how we imagine spaces.

In his novella *Heart of Darkness*, Joseph Conrad has his narrator Marlow describe how he felt about maps.[5] "Now," he says, "when I was a little chap I had a passion for maps. I would look for hours at South America, or Africa, or Australia, and lose myself in all the glories of exploration. At that time there were many blank spaces on the earth, and when I saw one that looked particularly inviting on a map (but they all look that) I would put my finger on it and say, 'When I grow up I will go there.'" This desire to know eventually leads Marlow to Africa and to the heart of the white space on the map along the coiling snake of the Congo River: a heart that he finds is full of the animal darkness of the human spirit. All of which is a poetic way of saying that Marlow, like his creator Joseph Conrad, made a habit of getting quite lost and then finding himself again—just for the hell of it.

Why do we do it? Why do humans go places, then make some record of that place, and then use that record to later describe and

---

[5] Actually, Marlowe narrates his own tale within the larger narrative told by an unnamed first-person ("I") speaker. A similar device is employed in Mary Shelly's *Frankenstein*, though in that case we know the speaker's name, **NAME**, (who is actually writing letters to his sister).

imagine what it must be (or have been) like? Even more bizarre is the fact that we make up places that no one has ever physically been. There are archives upon archives of maps of The Happy Hunting Grounds, Heaven, Hell, Purgatory, Narnia, Middle Earth, Xanth, and any other number of imaginary landscapes. In their *The History of Cartography Vol. I: Cartography in Prehistoric, Ancient, and Medieval Europe and the Mediterranean*, J.B. Harley and David Woodward describe this interest in representing space this way: "Curiosity about space—no less than about the dimension of time—has reached from the familiar immediate surroundings to the wider space of the earth and its celestial context. On another plane, men and women have explored with the inward eye the shape of sacred space and the realms of fantasy and myth. As visual embodiments of these various conceptions of space, maps have deepened and expanded the consciousness of many societies" (xv). This is to say maps not only describe or render spaces in virtual form, but they also create spaces in the imaginary landscape of a society. Maps help us understand who we are as a people and as individuals. Maps serve as the space for the cultural imagination to work and grow as they not only represent spaces but define what spaces may exist.

Take Marlow's concern with the blank spots on the map of Africa. What exists there within those borders put down with ink by Europeans from their ships sailing along the coasts? I believe the whole point of Marlow's story is that the making of the map, the act of exploring and filling in of the names and courses of the rivers, the charting of hills and mountains, and the dots with names that indicate villages and cities and points of interest, *creates* something as much as it *describes* something and in creating something new, such as the European capitalist version of African reality, something else is destroyed or diminished, such as a native populations' understanding of their territory as a spiritual space.

I have no desire to head into political territory here and enter into a digression on the evils of colonialism or post-colonial angst; rather, the point I am trying to make is that maps are not simply powerful tools for exploration that describe our world, they also serve to make the world of our understanding. Americans grow up seeing American maps and Russians are educated on very different maps, and this greatly affects our view of the world (in philosophical terms, our "weltanschauung").

Take me, for example. I consider myself an educated person with a quite broad base of knowledge. In college I studied political science, world literature, philosophy, and several foreign languages. Many of these studies included heavy doses of geography for which I was sometimes tested on. I distinctly remember filling in the various countries of South America and Europe on more than one test. I have also travelled the world some and learned many interesting things about the prejudices of everyday life. Yet, I once vehemently asserted to my partner that my home state of Texas was approximately the size of Brazil. I was, of course, completely wrong. Brazil, the fifth largest country in the world, is 8,511,965 square kilometers (5,289,090 square miles) in size to Texas' relatively tiny 696,200 square kilometers (or 268,820 square miles). How could I have made such a mistake? Is it true that Texans have an inflated view of themselves and their state?

Well, yes, actually. For a moment my internalized cultural geography as a Texan superseded my internalized cultural geography as a world citizen. I felt silly, of course, confronted as I was by a group of very amused international friends, but I also felt intrigued. Of course I knew Brazil is larger than Texas in actual square miles. How could I not? I knew it and yet I also knew something else—Texas is, partly by self-acclaim, "larger than life," particularly to those raised in the Texas educational system where state history is a strong part of the public education curriculum throughout. I had certainly seen massive images of Texas in textbooks and on walls and in films. Brazil was just a tiny country in a black and white map on my Spanish test. I was certainly factually wrong (and, under the circumstances, very badly wrong) but I was also culturally correct: for many Texans, Texas is bigger than just about anything.

Maps are fascinating; at least to me, because they are not just an extension of the body (strictly speaking, a tool like a hammer or pickaxe) but also an extension of self-perception, point-of-view, and imagination. The map extends the eyes by extending vision, but it not only allows the viewer to see a distant place and/or from a different angle, but to see that place *as imagined* or *remembered* and from a *disembodied perspective.*

Tool-making extends the body out into the world. Visual art places the human body within the realm of tools. Cartography then frees the body from the constraints of time and place: cartography is the first *disembodied* art form. That may not sound like much, but I will attempt to explain why this technology is so terribly important for our psychology and our history.

Imagine: we are a band of hunters standing on a plain. We have traveled this way many times and know the layout of the land. Ahead is a small hill. To the left a creek bed that is dry because it has not rained in a long time. To the right stands a clump of trees. Our prey—a small band of ibex none the worse for wear in the drought—wanders from the trees towards the hill chomping at small dried blades of grass. They are eating. We need to eat. But we know that if we get too close to them they will see us and smell us and run away. How do we sneak up on them? Or, how do we trap them so that one of us might get in a good shot? We only need one of the ibex after all, though several would certainly be better. Our stomachs are growling and there are babies crying back at the huts.

I look forward and point, finger extended towards the left of the hill indicating "We should go that way, around the hill." You know what I mean because my hand indicates the direction. I might even twiddle my fingers back and forth like little legs to give you more of a clue as to what I mean. This behavior is not particularly sophisticated, but it gets the job done. I could even split the group up in the same manner: "You three go that way, the rest of us this way. We will catch them in a crossfire in the middle."

All this is easy enough if we know the lay of the land and what lies beyond the hill. Even more importantly we *remember* (from the Latin *rememorārī* composed of the prefix "to go back" [re-] and "memory" or "mind" [*memor*], essentially mental time travel) what the terrain is like and can *imagine* (from Latin *imāgo* meaning "imitation") being there again. The terrain we remember is not actual terrain but an internal representation of it. The terrain has been internalized. As complex as all that might sound, however, even tiny white mice can be taught to memorize a maze for food and the situation we now find ourselves in is just a larger more complicated, less defined sort of maze. I have been this way before. I know what I should do. I can see myself, *remember*, doing it and can follow that memory. I can fashion myself in that place through a purely mental act by recreating the space and place and my physical presence solely in my mind: I remember the image and thereby recreate it, fashion it anew.

Back at the huts: I cannot go hunting today because I injured my foot on a sharp rock, so I have decided to stay home from the hunt and try to make something that will protect me from the burning pain every time I take a step. Not having any antiseptic, I will probably die from infection in the wound in any case, but I don't know that yet, so I am sitting around playing with pieces of hide and trying to lash them to my foot. I want to send you hunting instead as a runner has just returned and informed me that ibex are munching their happy way along towards the hill.

I describe the hill to you, the creek bed, the trees and my plan to capture the ibex in a crossfire. Even though I am not going with you, I can see how it should work because I have been there before. You don't seem to understand me. It is very hot today and you are obviously sleepy. You need a strong cup of coffee, but that hasn't been invented yet either. So, frustrated, I decide to draw you a simple picture in the dirt as I remember the terrain. Hill. Creek bed. Trees. Ibex. "Ah," you say, "right." What I have done is to remember my own body in a particular space and then externalize or represent that space with a crude drawing to help *you* remember the terrain. If you happen to have never been there before then it will be my drawing you remember as you try to match it to an external reality somewhere vaguely "that way."

If I am a terrible artist, I should try for a distinguishing feature: for example the hill is shaped like a woman's breast (and thus an epic poem is born). In any case, you might get lost if I do not communicate properly. This is what Swiss linguist Ferdinand de Saussure (1857-1913) was trying to explain with his famous triangle. In brief, communication has three parts: 1) transmitter, 2) the message, and 3) the receiver. For example, spoken communication has 1) a speaker, 2) the words combined into sentences, and 3) the listener. The speaker has an intention to communicate, frames the words and speaks them, and the listener then interprets or decodes the message. Things can go wrong at any stage in the process—I might not have a clear thought, choose vague words, and the listener might speak another language all together, and so on. For effective communication to take place, all three of these stages must be working in concert, and even then there are invariable misunderstandings and miscommunications. So amazingly difficult is communication, in fact, especially considering the great proliferation of languages, that the philosopher Baruch Spinoza (1632-1677) asserted that no one really communicates anything at all. However, we are going to be a bit more optimistic and hope that I can devise a map (my "text" for communicating) that will get the hunters to where they need to go.

As a form of communication, my representation of the hill attempts to visually express the location as I remember it from my own bodily experience of being there. Though it demonstrates a passing similarity to cave paintings (which have been considered as simple maps by some scholars) the main difference is in intent. Maps may describe spaces for a variety of reasons, but all maps imply a *verb tense* in the sense that they mark what *was* (past), what *is* (present), or what *may be* (future). If cave painting is history, then we might consider it a type of map. If it is predictive, we also might consider it a type of map, but if, as Davis Lewis Williams has argued, it is *descriptive* then it is visual art and not a type of cartography. The space exists, the wall itself is the space, and the artist is merely "highlighting" what is "already there"—at least to his or her eyes. There is for example, a significant difference between cave painting and one of what is arguably the earliest known maps, that of Çatalhöyük in Turkey (circa 6200 bce). If the image truly is a map, and there is some significant argument that it is not a town plan but a leopard or leopard-skin costume, then the image demonstrates a clear shift from first-person perspective and this is one of the defining characteristic of what most people would agree is a "map" rather than a "drawing" or "painting." The image seems to be, particularly in artist enhancements, a town plan seen from above including the image of a nearby volcano. Likewise, in the caves at Lascaux, there are spots that have been identified as stars. If they are stars, then they would arguably be maps, though with a shift in location only (from the sky to a cave ceiling) and not one in perspective—I look up and see the stars then, later, look up and draw what I remember. Much more likely, I believe, is the Lewis-Williams' argument that the "stars" in cave paintings are the result of optical illusions caused by heightened states of awareness (i.e. a trance). Regardless of which contestant for the first map wins out in the professional literature (if one ever does), by the time we clearly are dealing with what we can all agree is a "map" we are dealing with the demonstrated ability to imagine disembodied perspectives. Humans have learned, or acquired, or discovered, or wandered blindly into the ability to disembody the imagination. Rather than seeing a woman in a rock or seeing animals in stone shapes, rather than projecting ones' imagination *onto* something, cartography indicates the ability to imagine being someplace you currently are not or have never been.

The Catal Hoyuk "map" (c. 6200 bce).

Even fairly simple perspective maps have a change in perspective. If I draw a map with me standing on a hill waiting for ibex to pass, my imagined body will not be in proper proportion to the hill nor to the trees nor ibex (vanishing point perspective was still thousands of years away.) In fact, if I were actually seeing what I have drawn—an image of the plain from above—"I" would be floating in the air. There is a simple answer for this—I am not able to draw perspective properly. The same is true of this map of Çatalhöyük. This is, as it were, an impossible viewpoint for a human being short of having some sort of flying machine (which may be partially responsible for all the arguments for an alien intelligence having visited Earth in the past). The map is two-dimensional showing a flattened mountain and the street plan from above, what we now call "bird's eye view," but it is lacking in any depth.

But where is the "viewer," the person who sees the city from above? Where is the body that holds the eye as they look down on the hill? Looking at the map, if this were what I was actually seeing I would be floating in space somewhere: an impossible place where only birds can go and not be burned by the sun. The map maker has *imagined* his "self" (or perception) outside of his usual bodily experience and range of vision. It seems quite possible that bad art (what I should, rather, call the use of symbol rather than representation) has led the map maker to create an impossible bodily position. He has gone, in his mind, where no man can go. He has become, he has made himself, disembodied . . . and more. This is how the gods must see! Even the most simple of modern maps now require that incredible bird's-eye view perspective. We might think of the common football (of the American variety) playbook with the X's and O's and lines indicating the direction the players should run. Which brings us to another interesting point because once we are able to imagine the 3rd person perspective; we have the ability to represent the passage of time with successive maps.

Maps may not have always been around, but cartography is certainly a very old human technology and it operates as the marker for the ability of humans to use imagination to attain a disembodied perspective and to transmit and receive that perspective via symbolic images. Thus, whatever else the map may be, we may assert that the map is a tool that represents the conjunction of observation, perception, memory, representation, imagination, and communication. Obviously, maps are based in some sort of observation, and what we call perception is the act of understanding what one has observed. We might describe this act as the difference between "looking" and "seeing"; to look is to observe, to see is to perceive or to look closely by which we mean to observe and think critically. The map further relates to memory because we either must recall what has been seen or sketch what is being seen. In the latter case the map functions as a primary memory translatable to other viewers. But even in this case, the image must first pass through the map maker's mind and be translated to the page. In both cases, the map is a recorded observation of some sort, even if, as we shall see, the observation originates in imagination.

The map is, of course, also a form of representation. Like the Woman of Willendorf, the map is an externalization of an internalized vision or truth. Just as the carver of the Venus knew about (saw in the flesh) real women, the map maker also sees real hills and dales and bushes and ibex and bison. But the map, like the carving, is not a realistic, or photographic, image but an expressive image that both reduces the detail and increases the symbolism, however unintentionally; though there is little doubt that the impulse behind the creation of images is itself symbolic.[6] The map is not intended *to be the thing* but *to represent the essence of the thing*: to embody its virtues. The importance of this step should not be misunderstood. As Harley writes, "The development of the map, whether it occurred in one place or at a number of independent hearths, was clearly a conceptual advance—an important increment to the technology of the intellect—that in some respects may be compared to the emergence of literacy or numeracy."[7]

---

[6] "As images they [maps] evoke complex meanings and responses and thus record more than factual information on particular events and places." J.B. Harley and David Woodward, "Preface," in *The History of Cartography Vol. I: Cartography in Prehistoric, Ancient, and Medieval Europe and the Mediterranean*, ed. J.B. Harley and David Woodward (Chicago: University of Chicago Press, 1987. xv-xxi) xv.

[7] J.B. Harley "The Map and the Development of the History of Cartography" in *The History of Cartography Vol. I: Cartography in Prehistoric, Ancient, and Medieval Europe and the Mediterranean*, ed. J.B. Harley and David Woodward (Chicago: University of Chicago Press, 1987. 1-12) 4-5.

Imagination is that individual inexplicable leap that makes all the others possible. Imagination lifts the body above the plain, makes the eye fly even into the heavens, gives the artist the "God's eye view" and makes them able to see beyond what mortal eyes can see. To imagine is to see more clearly, but also to see what cannot usually be seen. Imagination is the "divine spark" of creation. As Arthur H. Robinson phrases it, "The use of a reduced, substitute space for that of reality, even when both can be seen, is an impressive act in itself; but the really awesome event was the similar representation of distant, out of sight, features. The combination of the reduction of reality and the construction of an analogical space is an attainment in abstract thinking of a very high order indeed, for it enables one to discover structures that would remain unknown if not mapped."[8]

Sigmund Freud, a pessimistic psychologist at the best of times, believed that all creation comes from dissatisfaction, or the experience of pain and suffering, and on this point I am inclined to agree as I can imagine what it must have felt like to *want* that illusive ibex for dinner, to see how it should be done, and to have a bunch of yahoos with me who just can't seem to do their parts right. I imagine this experience being rather like suddenly finding your arms and legs are no longer working. Certainly there are lots of animals that get by with a minimum of communication and everyone still flocks as they should (or almost everyone). That is what we call instinct: hardwired behavior that can lead to groups working together as a unit. But as instinct started to wane in the human animal, for whatever reason—dissatisfaction seems the likely culprit—communication became increasingly important to keep the rabble on the same page.

Ants work together, not by what we would call "choice" or even a perceived "necessity," but because that is what ants *do*. Humans work together because they *have to* by which I mean that we have feelings that drive us towards behaviors that are counter-productive

---

[8] Arthur H. Robinson, *Early Thematic Mapping in the History of Cartography* (Chicago: University of Chicago Press, 1982) 1.

to individual, or even collective, survival (what Freud called thanatos or "the death drive"). Ironically, according to Freud, this very dissatisfaction, the ability to feel dissatisfied due to a perceived *future* pleasure, is the basis for what we call "civilization".

We see this same idea in evolutionary theory: the grumpier and more prone to dissatisfaction a species is, the more highly evolved, more complex, it is likely to be or become. We call this tendency towards bitchiness, and note the word we use from the female canine who grumbles and growls and howls, "striving". We might say that ants are always *trying* and that humans are always *striving*. In any case, this talent to be unhappy, which, of course, also brings "happiness" into being as its dialectical opposite, is at the core of our psyche and the driving force of the human animal. We try to communicate because we are in general unhappy with what others are doing. We want to tell them to do something else: we want to say "No". When that does not seem possible our lives become more complex and we have to ask them what they are doing and why: "What the heck are you doing?" Then, if we pass that hurdle we have to explain what we want: "Stop waving your arms like an idiot and sneak up the creek bed, you dufus."

Essentially, we must draw others into our pain; and, as they say, pain is a matter of perspective, so we must draw others into our perspective so they can feel our pain and see the problem. Enter the map: "*This* is you, and *this* is the creek bed. Crawl. Kill ibex. Get it?" Thus, we cross the boundary of primary first-hand experience restricted to a particular time and place and enter into the realm of recorded experience that may be remembered and forecasted.

Thus, the map also operates as a tool of time, though it does not demonstrate the movement of time itself as does narrative to be discussed later. The map may represent what was, is, or what will be. In this function it serves both a practical function as recorded experience and a mystical function as the act of map making itself becomes an act of perceiving the past and the future of ownership through the ability to render. As if from a tall tower, the owner of the map can see the world and lay claim to all the eye beholds. Thus, the map becomes a commodity and a tool of conquest.

If one can represent something, one can seem to own it rather like one owns the car by having the keys. If we can represent heaven, then we can own that too, because we will be the ones who know, and can show, the way. There is with maps, as Harley writes, "an immediacy about the message in a map that makes it more readily perceived than knowledge encoded in other ways. . . . It has been said that maps have an 'extraordinary authority' even when they are in error, that may be lacking in other forms of images."[9] It allows us to imagine fantastic places that have never been, or at least have never been anywhere outside the map itself and the minds of those who gaze upon it. One of my favorite authors, J.R.R. Tolkien was, by his own admission, fascinated with maps from the time he was a boy, and from this fascination he created worlds and histories and peoples to live in them and languages for them to speak. Now we can see Middle Earth on the big screen and on the computer screen in the MMO game version and, even if it looks strikingly like New Zealand, it is indeed a whole other world made by us and for us.

Indeed, I probably have a better working knowledge of the geography of Middle Earth than I do of the United States. Some might think that is pathetic, irreverent, irreligious, or just plain geeky, but I think this is an essential trait of the human condition. After imagining and making bodies, we imagine the spaces for them to occupy. Some of these spaces are practical, some mythological or mystical or magical, still others fantastical, but we imagine them nevertheless and physically and mentally occupy them. In fact what we commonly call "culture" is based in our interactions with mapped cognitive terrains. We all have maps in our heads that chart the spaces in our lives. This is part of who we are as human beings.

---

[9] J.B. Harley "The Map and the Development of the History of Cartography" in *The History of Cartography Vol. I: Cartography in Prehistoric, Ancient, and Medieval Europe and the Mediterranean*, ed. J.B. Harley and David Woodward (Chicago: University of Chicago Press, 1987. 1-12) 1. Harley cites Arthur H. Robinson's "The Uniqueness of the Map," (*American Cartographer* 5 [1978], 5-7) and Kenneth E. Boulding's *The Image* (Ann Arbor: University of Michigan Press, 1956, 65-68) as examples of philosophical inquiries into the authority of the map.

The power of the map is not simply the power of representation, but the power to create a cognitive social space for a culture to occupy and express itself. The map speaks of bodies and spaces at a particular time. It may even speak, as does Dante's map of Hell in *The Inferno* or Tolkien's Middle Earth, of places imagined. But what the map cannot do on its own is *tell the story*—as much, as it might imply it, the map is locked in time. Which brings us to the third virtual discipline: after bodies and spaces comes the narrative. After all, once we find and kill that ibex we have to tell the tale.

Four: Inventing Time

Gilgamesh was a terrible and mighty king who ruled over the land of Uruk (in what is now modern day Iraq) sometime around 2700 bce. We know of Gilgamesh in part because his name is listed in the Sumerian kings list.[10] Even more importantly, however, his story is told in what is one of the oldest known recorded narratives: *The Epic of Gilgamesh*.[11] The most complete version of the tale was discovered by the British archeologist Austen Henry Layard in 1849 and has been dated to around the 7th century bce, but other pieces of the epic discovered at various locations in a variety of languages and dialects, date from 2150-2000 bce. By comparison, the oldest recorded samples of the Iliad date from 200 bce and are believed to be from texts dating as early as 800 bce; and the earliest existing versions of the Old Testament or Torah date from around 200 bce and are believed to derive from texts estimated to originate as early as 1000 bce. There may be disputes about the origin dates of our oldest stories, but *The Gilgamesh* is demonstrably amongst the oldest written narratives and arguably contains pieces of the oldest mythological stories ever told.

Like many epic heroes, Gilgamesh is at least half-god, and this status sets him apart from the common people. Even the aristocracy that serves him directly fear him. Unfortunately, as the story goes, Gilgamesh is so isolated from others that he becomes dangerously bored, and a bored god-king is never a good thing. As the story goes, "the men of Uruk muttered in their houses, 'Gilgamesh sounds the tocsin for his amusement, his arrogance has no bounds day or night. No son is left with his father, for Gilgamesh takes them all, even the children; yet the king should be a shepherd to his people. His lust leaves no virgin to her lover, neither the warrior's daughter

---

[10] In the past is was generally assumed that the list contained both mythological and historical kings and that Gilgamesh was mythological. However, recent scholarship asserts that while many of the feats of Gilgamesh told in the tale are fantastical, Gilgamesh, like Odysseus and Agamemnon, may have been a historical figure.

[11] The most complete version is from the 7th c. bce, however, the earliest known versions (found in partial form) date from 2150-2000 bce.

nor the wife of the noble". The people can do little but pray to the gods that Gilgamesh will once again behave like their true King and shepherd. So, hearing their lament, Aruru, the goddess of creation, made an equal for Gilgamesh out of the earth and named him Enkidu. Enkidu, who is covered all over his body with matted hair and has long hair like a woman's, knows nothing of civilization and runs wild with the animals. Perhaps the first eco-terrorist, Enkidu destroys the hunters' traps, but they devise a plan the catch him. "Go to Uruk, find Gilgamesh, extol the strength of this wild man. Ask him to give you a harlot, a wonton from the temple of love; return with her, and let her woman's power overpower this man. When he next comes down to drink at the wells she will be there, stripped naked; and when he sees her beckoning he will embrace her, and then the wild beasts will reject him."

As plans go to catch a wild man, I must admit that sending for a harlot would probably not be the first thing that would come to my mind. I certainly cannot see hunting for Bigfoot with a prostitute outside the framework of a really bad horror flick. However, I have to admire the Adam and Eve simplicity of the idea: if you want to civilize a man, to bring him from the state of nature into the society of work and responsibility, what you need is a woman. And here we find ourselves staring back through time to the Woman of Willendorf for the unnamed prostitute, the "child of pleasure" as Gilgamesh calls her, does appear to Enkidu naked and she is the symbol of sexual pleasure and fecundity. They make love for six days and seven nights. Afterwards, the animals do, in fact, reject Enkidu and he returns to the woman who prepares him to be a man. She shaves his body and teaches him to eat bread and drink wine. Enkidu helps the shepherds by killing lions and is generally happy being a man until one day a man shows up with the news that Gilgamesh has claimed the kingly right to have sex with all new wives before their husbands. Angered, Enkidu declares that he will go and challenge Gilgamesh and change the old order.

After a fierce battle, Gilgamesh and Enkidu become friends and adventure together until, one day, Enkidu is injured by the forest demon Humbaba and, eventually, dies. Gilgamesh is inconsolable and wanders the desert in search of the power to bring Enkidu back to life and along the way learns the lesson that lead him to become a wise and fair ruler for his people. We do not have the space to cover the whole tale here, of course, but it is a fascinating tale full of events that resonate throughout the history of world mythology and literature which is part of the reason it endures beyond the first 40 pages or so of World Literature textbooks. Though it spoiled the ending for me, I was pleasantly surprised, for example, to find that the *Star Trek: The Next Generation* episode "Darmock" (aired 30 Sept. 1991)[12] retells the tale of Enkidu, Gilgamesh, and Humbaba as the encounter between Captain Picard and an alien whose language is constructed solely from mythico-historical analogies. Thus something like "Gilgamesh and Enkidu at the Forest against Humbaba" would mean in English "Two friends who stand together against a common enemy even unto death".

My point here is that even our earliest recorded narratives still have the power to enthrall us in their worlds whether they be fiction, mythology, or history, or a combination of all three; and what we find enthralling about these tales are bodies moving through spaces over time. Thus, *The Gilgamesh* not only names, but physically describes, sometimes in minute detail, the people, animals, monsters, and gods who populate the tale. Like the Woman of Willendorf externalizes the thought of "Woman," so the *Epic of Gilgamesh* transmits the image of "Gilgamesh," and "Enkidu," and "the Harlot" who is also called "the Woman." I may not see the exact same Humbaba as you see, but we both see Humbaba nonetheless. This ability to transmit the image from one mind to another (albeit in altered form) is an evolved form of the artistry needed to make the Woman of Willendorf, but it is rooted in the same impulse and aims at a similar result.

Likewise, *The Epic of Gilgamesh* is a geography. It describes actual landscapes, mythological landscapes, and the socio-political terrain. Uruk was an actual place: a city-state with massive walls, a

---

[12] "Darmock" Episode 102. Writ. Joe Menosky, *Star Trek: The Next Generation* episode (aired 30 Sept. 1991)

palace, and a marriage house, all as described. Just like the Woman of Willendorf evolves into the unnamed prostitute, so the map evolves into the narrative terrain where we can imagine the spaces and their relative locations without an actual map before us or an actual person standing there telling us the way and pointing. Though narratives are not maps *per se*, they do not require the technique of representing and understanding representations, or renderings, of various points of view. In the case of *The Epic of Gilgamesh*, in order to read and understand the tale I must know who "I" am in relation to the "teller." In this case I am a "listener" hearing the recorded (written) voice of a "speaker." Though a linguist could explain more fully, there are elements of *The Gilgamesh* that have moved beyond the strictly verbal—the recording of spoken sounds—into what is often called "the literary," or the use of written language to its own artistic ends.

The mythical spaces in *The Gilgamesh* seem to adjoin the real spaces or to overlay them. "Heaven," for example, is not so much a place as is Mt. Olympus to the Ancient Greeks, but an overlaying space with access points (including dreams) through which the gods and their servants can pass. Likewise, the riverfront where Gilgamesh stays with a woman and almost gives up his quest seems more a state of mind than an actual place. Like the cave paintings at Lascaux, these "other worlds" seem to show through the walls of the mundane world. And, of course, the socio-political spaces cover all as the "terrain" of the tale exists in order to describe a society and its people and, thereby, to help create and maintain it. *The Gilgamesh* was, for its people, a nationalizing literature that helped create a mental terrain of connections between people (bodies) and places (or spaces). Which brings me to the point that *The Gilgamesh* does something more than simply put bodies in spaces and describe them, it engenders *time*, for with the invention of narrative (with the evidence that narrative had been invented) comes the invention of time as we know it.

Humans are the only animals that experience the world almost entirely through memory. Narrative engendered time as an asynchronous concept through the invention of past-tense where one can describe, through the act of speaking, actions which have already happened. In other words, narrative is a form of disembodied memory. Again, like the Venus of Willendorf and the map, narrative is essentially perspective sharing. Like the map, narrative allows a speaker to recreate in words events of the past or even to give verbal form to events that transpire solely in the mind that originate in dreams or imagination. Thus narrative incorporates both the functions of the made body by describing the actions of bodies not currently seen and the function of the map by creating (again in words) spaces not currently accessible. Body, space, and time meet in the narrative.

Returning to our ibex episode from the previous chapter, we might recall that we left the hunters heading out to find dinner. Upon their return I notice, however, that they have no ibex and I am clearly distraught. After all, my stomach is rumbling. The hunters see my reaction and interpret my body language correctly as frustration. They have a desire to explain what happened. One hunter points at the map still lingering in the dirt then uses his fingers on the sides of his head to mimic an ibex and another plays himself as a hunter. The hunter follows the ibex unaware, closes on it and prepares to leap. However, a third hunter leaps out from imaginary bushes and growls fiercely—a lion! And the hunter feigns running away.

This acting out of a past event is just a short step from telling the tale in words, but the effect is the same: for narrative to operate we must have the capacity to "make" bodies (either graphic, emulated, or described verbally) imagine and share spaces, and have a clear enough concept of time to understand that "before" can be drawn into the "now." Thus, in demonstrating their story to me the hunters have "explained" what happened using virtual bodies, spaces, and times. Considering the centrality of our own bodies in the making of tools, art, and maps it should not be surprising that our bodies also serve as the basis for narrative.

We see in *The Gilgamesh*, then, the basic technologies needed for all human endeavor—the ability to describe a body moving through space and time. This is the basis for all of what we now call "the disciplines" from physics to psychology to neurology to theology, and on and on. From quantum mechanics to Harley-Davidson mechanics, we all use the same basic building blocks to describe and teach and learn what we do: bodies moving through space and time.

But why did we start to tell tales in the first place? No one knows when or why humans began to tell stories, but it is safe to say that what we think of as "humans" have always told stories because we are, as fantasy author and satirist Terry Pratchett writes, *homo narens*, the ones who tell tales. This is to say that humans have been making up reality since they first invented a rudimentary language. What we do not know will be answered; the wide gaps in knowledge will be filled with, as we say in Texas, "bullshit".

Why? Because despite what some say, as long as humans are thinking self-reflexive beings, what we do not know *can* hurt us. Therefore, we come up with tools to explain how things work and predict what will happen around the next bend—make some sense of the world that is so earnestly trying to kill us off one by miserable one. It is certainly to our evolutionary advantage to use every tool (which quickly becomes most of everything in the world) at our disposal to prolong our lives and reduce suffering. And most human suffering comes from unfulfilled desire, which is perhaps the one thing that Jesus, Buddha, Marx, Freud, Jung, Lacan and all the rest all agreed upon. Weaving verbal sense out of it all—creating a verbal virtual reality—eases the pain of living a brute life. Stories (narratives) ease the physical pain of life by predicting future events and outcomes based upon past experience. Something happens to me, I tell you about it, you tell Fred and then Fred one day finds himself in a similar situation and he does what I did, improves upon it, and (if he lives to tell the tale) an action evolves into a Neat Idea.

This sense of increased security, the ability of the narrative to increase our chances for survival, makes us feel more secure and less afraid. We *believe* in the power of narrative and, therefore, feel better because we worry less about the millions of things there are to worry about when one is a self-reflexive mammal. Eventually, this belief in the *power* of the narrative is confused with belief in the *subject* of the narrative and a fetish object is born. For example, the short narrative "I put my doohickey down here over his erect thingamajig, we bounced around a bit, and then my tummy grew and nine months you came out" is a useful narrative for explaining a person's origin (what is called an "etiology" meaning "where things came from") and for teaching the basics of procreation. Not to mention that it is a fairly complex observation on cause and effect that is considerably far along from the instinct to copulate. But, by associated logic and humans' need to explain what they do not know (filling in those "why" gaps again), this short narrative can quickly morph into a phallus cult or cult of the woman where the instructional power of the narrative form is hidden and supplanted by the subject of the narrative. If anything is magical it is the *power of story* and not the run-of-the mill penis and vagina and (sorry kid!) all too mundane human baby. Let's face it, the so-called miracle of birth is not the real miracle because every living thing on the planet does that including worms, and they would be doing it even if we weren't around to call it miraculous. I daresay worms do not find worm sex "miraculous." What the real miracle is, the origin of the "miracle" itself, is that we can tell the tale.

Five: Ruling the World

One day, my partner and I were sitting on a stone bench in Boboli gardens. Boboli is a massive park of trees, bushes, fountains and sculptures in Florence, Italy. We were surrounded by both life-sized sculptures (one of the main attractions of Boboli) and real breathing and sweating people. It was very hot that day—well over 100 degrees. I was fascinated by the juxtaposition of the hard, closed flesh of the stone statues and the more porous grotesque bodies of the visitors all drinking water, eating moldering sandwiches with wilted lettuce and tomatoes, and sucking on dripping gelati or multi-colored Italian ices. The lines by the restrooms were formidable. I could not help but wonder what the pristine sculptures must think (if they could think) of this mass of humanity come into their domain and how we must seem quite a bunch of open leaky sacks of fluids as mouths were stuffed; sweat, feces, and urine excreted; and trashcans filled to brimming with cups and napkins and disposable dirty diapers. For hundreds of years these statues had stood immobile, beautiful, and pristine. Time must seem very long for them, I thought, and the lives of men must seem all too short. Why had we come to look on these stone gods at all? It seemed we had come to that verdant inferno to deny everything we are, to worship form over content and the solid over the fluid flesh. This is, perhaps, what we aspire to be: beautifully carved rock made by the hands of man, chiseled out of granite and (seemingly) inconsiderate of Time.

There was a child of little more than two years playing in the rough-hewn gravel around the fountain where we sat. He was certainly unimpressed by the statues, though he was fascinated by stones nonetheless. As we watched he would spread his tiny reddening legs wide, look expectantly about him, and then drag handfuls of the hot white gravel into his crotch area. When he had a rather tidy pile he would stand, take aim over the pile and then promptly plop right down on top of it. The act of forcefully sitting on the pile, naturally, flattened it out so that when he stood again, the pile was gone and he would dance and clap in jubilation calling to his parents "*Mira!*" ("Look!") in Spanish. He repeated this procedure over and over again, each time showing the same pleasure at the "disappearance" of the pile of rocks. It occurred to me that simply flattening the pile with his behind was not really what the child had in mind at all, and I was reminded of Freud's discussion the "*fort/da*" game where a child acted out his mother's leaving his immediate sight with a doll. The child I was observing could not see what was happening below him when he plopped down. Nor was he piling rocks beside him and then patting them down. No. Quite clearly the child was pulling the hot rocks towards his crotch and anus then forcing himself down on top of them repeatedly and witness a pile "gone," when he looked, "to somewhere." Where had the pile gone?

It seemed to me then, as far as the child was concerned, the pile of rocks had gone inside of his body. He could see them there before all piled up, feel the pressure as he sat forcefully upon them, and then see that the pile was no longer there. He was trying, I thought, through some infantile desire, such as putting things into the mouth as all children do, to incorporate them into his own flesh. No doubt the sensation of the rocks against the flesh must have given him much the same impression one has when taking a hot bath, that as the heat works its way inside, we are somehow being filled with the water (an observation not entirely inaccurate as we are mostly water to begin with, and water does seep into our skin, albeit slowly, as anyone who has ever had "Trench Foot" knows all too well). This was a game with only one rule: consume the world and, thereby, become the world.

We could certainly discuss Sigmund Freud and the anal stage here, and the little boy would be about the right age, but the important point is that the physical pleasure the little boy obviously feels from the heat and the pressure of the rocks on his buttocks and anus (if pain exceeded pleasure he would not repeat the action) is superseded by the pleasure in the virtual body: in this case a body that can magically take an enormous amount of rocks inside. After all, things come out of there, as the child well knows, so why can't things go in? The reverse is the pleasure children take in spitting out things that go into the mouth. The psychological joy is not in the physical body but in the projection of a body (with rocks inside) that cannot be properly said to exist in biological terms.

All play, at the most basic and primal level, in an interaction with the world whereby we express via complicated reflexive processes both our individuality (through action) and our desire towards completion/dissolution (passivity). We move rocks, thus exercising control over the world, and then try to incorporate them, which is a denial our separateness from the world. The little boy did not want to make the rocks submit to his will, as we might assume were his simply flattening the pile, he wanted to become them, to have that hardness and warmth inside. And here the rest of us were just looking at statues.

Or were we simply looking? These statues are a more complex case, certainly, wrapped up as they are in history and aesthetics and the arts, and yet they represent the same desire at a broader cultural level. The artists controls the stone, gives it form, and the culture internalizes it and becomes it. On a primal psychological lever, the sculptures of Western Civilization that we all so admire are so many rocks we are shoving up our asses. Stop for a moment and think. How does a fine piece of art make you feel? Warm. How does a beautiful body of either sex make you feel? Warm. How do we describe that feeling? We say "I lost myself in it." The French psychiatrist-psychoanalyst Jacques Lacan (1901-1981) is certainly right on this point: We live in an imaginary realm of solid, individual, bodies and desire what our feelings tell us is the actual "real world" where all that individuality goes away and we return to the impossibly lost world (what Lacan terms the pre-mirror stage) where there is no "I," no "me," and therefore, no "you". Lacan's contemporary, the French existentialist philosopher Jean Paul Sartre (1905-1980) described this feeling of pain in separateness as "Hell is the Other" (sometimes translated as "Hell is other people"). Humans are defined completely by this paradox of desire to be and not to be as individuals, which emerges again in Freud's terms as Eros (the erotic drive or "pleasure principle") and Thantos (or "death drive"). Looking at the rocks we made, we see our desire to be unmade (death) and remade (rebirth) as the Other in an infinite cycle until we come to be one with everything: what Lacan termed "the Real".

At the end of the garden is a famous statue of Bacchus that seems to make some attempt to break down that division between the perfect concept of a body and the open bodies of real men and women. At first Bacchus seems truly hideous by comparison to the other statues. Bacchus's mouth is grotesquely open. His fat corpulent stomach extrudes over his stubby sex and withered legs. This is a statue in reverse, a statue that gazes upon itself like we gaze upon the Venus de Milo or the David. As part of their social training, children of almost every culture engage in forms of play that mimic more adult behaviors and responsibilities. Some of these are clearly modeling behaviors such as "playing house" or "doctor" or "cowboys and Indians" where the rules for the play are culled from observation of the world. It is, in effect, an interpretive act (this is the way adults behave) and a discipline (this is the way we should or will behave). The important point here is that human beings acquire behaviors and thought patterns through modeling behaviors.

Baccus, Boboli Gardense, Florence, Italy.
Courtesy Wikimedia Commons.

In the simplest of societies (or the least complex) one's role within the society is clearly defined from birth and is not usually subject to change as the necessities of the life of the group depend upon everyone doing their part. In the Mbuti pygmy tribe of the Congo region of Africa, for example, the most basic societal division among the persons are those who are too young to hunt, those who hunt, and those who are no longer able to hunt. Labor for the collective is then assigned accordingly and everyone has a clear role to play within the system. By necessity, gender differences are at an absolute minimum because every able-bodied hunter is needed on the hunt: males and females are treated the same except in those unremarkable cases when babies are born and need to be breast fed. Those tasks accomplished the female returns to her role as a hunter. Children also have their roles: they are to learn to work together in order to be hunters and they are keepers of the sacred fire because they are innocent and have not yet been "bloodied" on the hunt. The elderly have the task of tending the children when needed, training them, and preparing food. No one person has one job, but will cycle through the jobs of the tribe as age and ability allow. When you are a child you have a child's job, when you are an adult you hunt, and when you are older you tend the children and the camp. If you get sick or hurt, you rest. If you menstruate, you rest. If you have a baby, you rest and feed it until it can eat on its own.

Simple societies vary widely, of course, but what we see in the Mbuti is true of all of them: the role an individual is to play, the position one is to occupy in the society, is always clear with little to no ambiguity. In effect, each individual embodies the whole of the society as each individual will pass through all the stages and perform all the tasks required for the survival of the whole. "I" am "Mbuti" and that means I will do everything a Mbuti does as far as my body allows.

As societies become more complex, individuals tend to become more specialized. The necessary division of age is followed by the largely unnecessary division along sex-gender lines, which is, in turn, followed by the division of labor. One person may be a better hunter than another who is better at pottery, so they each spend the majority of their time doing what they do best and each contributes to the whole. Therefore, by the time we reach our earliest stories such as *The Epic of Gilgamesh* we see a division of labor into kings, hunters, shepherds, harlots, and so on. In this case, the individual becomes more closely associated with the products of their work and may become more skilled through the benefit of added training to improve their *technique*. This strengthening of technique leads to new and better technologies—a better pot, a better spear, new hunting and fishing techniques, and etc.—that make the overall society more productive and able to grow more rapidly and humans move from wandering tribes or bands into agrarian communities which are eventually able to support city-states. But what the society has gained in productivity the individual has lost in group identification. One is no longer simply a Mbuti (or with as many adjectives as possible, a Mbuti of hunting age who is male) but has now become a Mbuti *hunter* who will not experience what it means to be fully Mbuti, partaking in all the society's needs.

Furthermore, whereas the original division of labor between young, adult, and elderly implied a very limited hierarchy (everyone will be, is, or has been a hunter, just as everyone has been or is a child, and etc.) the tendency towards the creation of hierarchies increases exponentially with specialization. The male hunter, due to his increased skill at arms, can now bully the potter. Specialization also highlights the differences between genders: the woman's *primary* labor becomes childbearing in order to ensure the growth of the tribe and her *primary* concern becomes the protection of the child which, frees the male hunter from such worries. Thus it is that the male hunter-fighter class is the one that rises to the top of the heap in almost every case where specialization occurs and the "strong aggressive alpha-males" become the culturally preferred child and adult, the "best of the best" and everyone else becomes an "other," lesser, supportive being.

The best man of the hunting-fighting men then becomes the ruler of all people in his role as "protector." As the individual moves farther and farther from the center of the culture and no longer fully participates in the culture, they come not to embody the culture (all its virtues, all its stations) but rather they enact only a small fragment of the culture. Even the "King" is a specialist in ruling and no longer participates fully in the making of the culture he rules. Kings like Gilgamesh never make pots or tend children, and yet he administers all of these at the highest level. In essence the King, as the head of the specialized society, has come to symbolically represent the virtues of the culture without actually embodying them at all—the position of King (with a capital "K") is thus posited *as the culture itself,* and each particular body that happens to sit on the throne is simply a temporary manifestation. Thus the King is a virtual construction and each man who becomes King is merely an avatar, a body filled with the virtues of the society. When Gilgamesh wanders from his role of being a "shepherd to the people" they pray to the gods for him to realign himself with his true nature. Even as they list off their complaints about him, they affirm "yet this is the shepherd of the city, wise, comely, and resolute": in other words, a king who has not quite yet become King, not quite yet overcome with the virtues of King, not quite yet become virtual.

Kings are not the only lives that are virtual, however. All of us continue to play roles throughout our lives. We acquire many different roles as we move through our world, each with its own set of rules. With all these roles to play (beginning as far back as "child," "son," "daughter" or what have you) we must wonder where the original "me" is to begin with, and certainly with all of our modern self-help psychology it is amply apparent that we have become worried about where the "real me" has gone to if I can make statements like "I just don't feel like myself anymore," or, after therapy or certain drugs, I can "feel like myself." Who, exactly did we feel like before if not like ourselves? How can I not feel like me? That I can even ask those questions demonstrates that we, as a society (and particularly Westerners), have become increasingly aware, thanks at least in part popular psychology, that we play many roles, or what used to be called "wearing many hats," and that playing these many roles can have a profound impact on our psychology—in fact the roles may even be what we call our psychology or psyche.

Shifting social imperatives can also play a significant role in our feeling that we are no "real." Whereas kids can pick up roles and play with them like any other toy—today a cowboy, tomorrow a doctor, the next day a garbage man—adults feel pressured to clearly define themselves by one or more roles, and where it was not uncommon in past times for a person to essentially serve one significant role in their life (or a series of roles, one after another) such as "blacksmith" or "wife" ("husband" and "daughter" being minor side-roles comparatively), and were often even called by their job rather than their given name, the sheer number of roles has increased and the relative importance of each de-prioritized. When at work we are expected to act as if work is the most important thing (even if it is not) and when at home we are expected to act like our domestic life is the most important thing (when it may not be).

I know a woman of very strong of intellect and character who seems to have two very different lives: one in New York City where she works and one in Illinois which she calls "home". As a college professor and administrator, she works a nine-month schedule that would seem daunting to even the most hardened professor. She gives the great majority of her waking hours to the students, faculty, and college. On top of all that, she is an impeccable dresser as befits her role as an academic administrator. Then, for three months out of the year, more or less, she becomes a rural, family-oriented person living on the family farm. I truly envy her ability to compartment-alize her life into two clear-cut roles. I am certainly not capable of that level of distinction, and I suspect few of us are these days. As we shift from role to role we may become confused about what persona is the central one. "Who am I?" is the defining question of the postmodern era.

Partly this stems from the fact that the world has changed radically in a very short time. These days we can have many lives within one life. Though I am a college professor, I do not come from a family of academics, and yet I have become an academic by a meandering path that involved several other potential careers along the way: an infantryman in the military, a pre-law student, a newspaper columnist, a roofer, a waiter, a bartender, and etc. I am not a Smith from a family of blacksmiths, so to speak. This ability to change "professions" throughout our lives is both liberating and confusing.

We also have become a much more transient people. Without a close physical relationship to family and a life-long set of friends, it is understandable that we might continually feel the need to ask "Who am I?" in a world that does not tell us, or affirm, who we are. In fact we now live in a world that continually reinforces the fact that we do not know ourselves. Rather than an aging parent constantly reminding us that we are their children—the same children that played Cowboys and Indians in the barn and broke all the windows out in order to shoot the bad guys—we are now told by people we do not know that we can feel better and get more done if we only do Yoga, Tai-Chi, or Pilates, or take Xanax, Zoloft, or Zocor. These fix-alls (take Zoloft for example—a word already in my spell-checker when I bought this word-processing program) all imply that there is something quite wrong with who we are right now.

I am by no means implying that we return to the rigid roles of the past. Rather, we should be aware that the progression and proliferations of roles the individual subject may "play" has in part lead to the condition we refer to as the "postmodern subject" and much of the anxiety we now suffer stems from a culture caught in the latest round of "growing pains." It makes perfect sense that it is virtually impossible to know who or what you want to "be" if you don't know who you "are" and the person you are (when you do seem to know) is generally referred to in our culture as an "illusion" a "delusion" or a "sickness."

We live in a world where it has become almost impossible to be depressed for a few days without further worrying about our "condition." Our personalities used to solidify as we aged from dreaming of being a king to recognition that we had become, after all, a rather good blacksmith. Now, our potential selves diversify as we leave home and enter the larger world and, truth be told (and the pharmaceutical profits seem to support it), most of us don't like it one bit. And there is the rub, for the process of diversification of "the self" or "the subject" does not care if we like it or not. Processes do not care. Due to myriad factors described in virtually every discipline from evolution to complex dynamics to music theory to psychology, we are increasingly becoming multiple selves, and by the (perhaps outmoded) rules of psychology of the individual, this also means we are becoming sick. Putting one person on Prozac is like planting a solitary pole against the rising sea. The pole may not move for a while, but the water comes anyways. A much better plan would be to learn how to swim well: even more fun would be to learn how to surf! Ideally, we would learn to once again live in water, or even, eventually, become water itself.

But all that is, as my friend Geoff Klock (author of *How to Read Superhero Comics and Why* [2002] and *Imaginary Biographies* [2007]) says, "Intellectual hoo-ha." What all this means to me is that a Prozac (another word already in my spell-checker) Nation is a nation in denial of the essentially dynamic nature of the human biosphere and the universe we inhabit. As the universe gets larger, so do we: too large even for our own bodies. We do not feel alive. We feel lost somewhere in the system and unsure of what role to play. Perhaps that is why games are so appealing to us, because in the game we always know, or at least believe we know, the rules.

My partner, Ximena Gallardo C. is a cartoon fan with a fairly significant collection of *Pogo, Peanuts, Asterix, Lucky Luke, Cathy, Zits, Garfield, Life in Hell,* and *Doonesbury,* to name a very few. My favorite cartoon of the bunch, for psychological reasons that are probably obvious to everyone but me, is *Calvin and Hobbes*. One of the reasons I like *Calvin and Hobbes* that they are always inventing and playing games and they draw interesting philosophical conclusions from their play. My absolute favorite is "Calvinball"— an ever-evolving, 2 person, extravaganza of improvisation. As Calvin says "The only rule in Calvinball is that you can't play the same way twice!"[13] In the world of Calvinball anything goes as long as you can state the rule before you do something. All kids make up games, of course, but what I like about Calvinball is that it draws attention to the artifice of games and, by association, rule systems in general. Calvin is not a big fan of rules (particularly not in school) and thus Calvinball is the perfect expression of why he does not like rules: he sees through the arbitrariness of it all. Cartoonist Bill Waterson is suggesting through Calvin that, at a very fundamental level, most societal rules really are "just because" and that any meaning behind the rules, like in Calvinball, is ultimately based on mutual agreement. This is what we mean when we say "life is a game": though it might be more accurate, albeit less catchy, to say "social life, like a game right out of the box, is a system we are learning". We enter a society at birth, try to learn the rules as we go along and follow them for the most part (if we are not sociopaths), in some cases break the rules accidentally or clandestinely and hope not to get caught, and eventually achieve some sense of success.

This "game-ness" of life—the feeling that if we only understood the rules fully, we could "win"—indicates the difference between play and games. Many mammals engage in what we call "play". Play is part of how they learn the limits of their bodies as they are growing and learn how to be adults by emulating experiences (like hunting) that will help them be successful adults. What we call "games," however, are particular to humans and originate in *logistics*: the study of how to get things and people from here to there as efficiently as possible. Of course sometimes other things and people might be in our way from getting to there, so they would have to be moved as well: this is what we would call "war". Little wonder, then, that our earliest formalized games (including sports) seem based around skills needed for war and the movement and supply of fighting troops.

In fact, scholars are now suggesting that Mesopotamia, the origin of *The Epic of Gilgamesh*, held early versions of the Olympic games (now appropriately called The Gilgamesh Games) and one of

---

[13] Bill Watterson, *The Calvin and Hobbes 10th Anniversary Book* (Kansas City: Andrews and McMeel, 1995) 129.

the earliest examples of board games in the world, now called *The Royal Game of Ur*, dates to the First Dynasty of Ur (before 2500 bce) near Gilgamesh's home city of Uruk. I do not want to belabor the point here more than to say that written narratives, what we now consider to be organized sports, and board games all seem to originate at around the same time. This makes sense since all three are *simulation technologies*. In sports, at least originally, battle skills are clearly defined and are emulated in a non-lethal or reduced risk setting. Sports were, in a word, *practice* for war. Likewise, stories define events and give shape to reality and, like sports, stories are at heart instructional: listening to a story of the hero Gilgamesh and how he learned how to be a great king is a psychological *practice*. And games also originate with real world practices and seek to emulate them in an instructional way. All three activities are also *fun* because like their ancestor, spontaneous play, narratives, sports, and games are simulations removed from the very real mortal and psychological dangers of a harsh life.

The evolution of sports is, perhaps, not difficult to understand. If a soldier wanted to survive a battle he would practice throwing his javelin. Two soldiers throwing javelins, like two lion cubs stalking a bird, becomes a competition. A few thousands of years and billions of dollars later and we have the Olympics, the Super Bowl, and the World Cup. Throwing your javelin in practice is more fun than throwing it in battle (for most people anyways) because you are much less likely to die. Not dying is, in general, more fun than the other option.

The evolution of games might be a bit more difficult to understand; however, like sports, games probably originated from the same impulse as sports: to win at war. But whereas sports are based on individual or small team physical and mental performance, the simulation equivalent of the individual soldier or small unit, board games are simulations for the leaders of the units—what commands they should give to who, when they should give them, and why they should give them.

War games have probably been around as long as organized warfare and this is easy enough to understand. Once the battle plan moved beyond a few soldiers running wildly "over there" while screaming their lungs out, some sort of formal planning had to take place. One can well imagine the ancient general's frustration with drawing plans in the dirt with a stick and his commissioning of maps and tokens (and later figurines) to indicate the plan of a future attack, keep track of a current battle, and to recap a battle already won or lost. Though some of the oldest extant games, such as Senet and The Royal Game of Ur, are "race games" (or "get there first") with similarities to modern day backgammon, even these have roots in the movement of bodies from place to place and their primary instructional value is located therein.

The games with the most obvious direct connections to warfare (and the politics surrounding warfare) are the so-called "strategy games"—a term which implies that strategy is the main skill acquired through playing them, though certainly all games benefit from strategy or strategic planning. Having already reached a sophisticated level, ancient examples of strategy games include the oriental game Go (a game still played avidly in some sectors of the world today), Chaturanga from India (now often described as an ancestor to Chess), and, of course, the best known game in the world: Chess. According to Thomas B. Allen, some sources also attribute the war game Wei Hai to the Chinese philosopher-general Sun Tzu whose *The Art of War* (c. 500 b.c.) has served as a handbook for military generals and corporate moguls ever since. Wei Hai was perhaps the first game to feature rules for moving large units.[14]

The most important element of these early games for our discussion is the representation of individuals and units with markers or figurines, the invention of a virtual terrain (or map) often marked off with some type of grid, and the formalization of "rules" that simulate the real world to some degree. In modern chess, for example, the figures represent actual positions of power in medieval society: the King and Queen who rule, the Bishop who slides

---

[14] Thomas B. Allen "War Games" In *Reader's Companion to Military History* (Houghton Mifflin, http://college.hmco.com. Accessed 23 January 2004).

sideways rapidly sideways across the territory (like most politicians), the mounted Knight who moves rapidly to surround or outflank, the Pawn who is poorly trained and equipped (cannon fodder mostly) and cannot move very quickly, and the Castle that marks the boundary of one's territory by drawing straight lines (a more distinctly military version invented in Germany—pre 17th century—adopts more obviously military titles for the pieces).

As I previously asserted, the making of models to represent the human form marks our entrance into history. Nor is figure-making an ancient art lost in the deep impenetrable mists of time. As I have already stated, representation of the human form seems to be one of our defining characteristics, and the markers of our history attest to the progression of a never-ending series of human figures created for an incredibly wide range of purposes. It should come as no surprise, then, that with the invention of maps these same human figures or more easily made and transported markers reduced from the detail of the figurine to the most simplistic form of the square or oval, should find their way onto the miniature terrain. In the small pebble of the game Go we see the shape of the human head as seen from above. Looking down on these diminutive figures, men becomes like gods warring over the fate of a subspecies.

In these games one can kill without killing and win without winning, by which I mean that the rewards of winning the "battle" and the penalties for loosing are shifted from the body to the board and imagination. Whereas in a real battle bodies are wounded and opened and thereby serve as the indicator of the power of the winner (a physical inscription of one's power onto the body of another) the game abstracts these consequences to such a degree that the joy or pain one suffers from winning and losing is entirely psychological and most often no longer seems tied to its root in the rending open (or at least beating) of another body. Chess is like war but it is not war simply because the "bodies" are too abstracted for them to serve in the place of real soldiers. Though there are stories of games played in lieu of actual battle to decide the fates of the participants, nations generally do not engage in them.[15]

Perhaps the most interesting development from the map to the strategy-war game is the inclusion of rules that define a "world." These rules arose no doubt from an ever increasing need to move from simple strategy to more complex logistics. A band of several men, a rabble, is fairly easy to direct as a group. As strategies for hunting and war become more complex the need for long-term planning increases.

As Napoleon Bonaparte supposedly said, "An army moves on its stomach": which is to say that all those men need to be fed to stay in fighting shape. Logistics in this sense is about the requirements and limitations of bodies. How fast can trained soldiers move in a day? How fast can they move and still be able to fight efficiently? What are the different march rates for different types of units? How little food can they survive on? The lowest common denominator is of great interest to a general because the entire army essentially moves at the rate of the slowest unit, or one runs the risk of dangerous divisions in the units. Strength is in numbers, after all.

And then there are the different types of terrain and climates. The Romans built great roads for many reasons, not the least of which was the rapid movement of troops and supplies to where they were needed most. Roads reduce the difficulties of terrain to simply level ground, uphill, or downhill, only one of which is any significant problem for an army on the go. As far as weather is concerned, extreme heat and cold require extreme measures. The Russians are well known for allowing invasions to enter their territory and then simply waiting until the winter hits and the supply lines dwindle. Napoleon and Hitler are only two more famous examples of complete failures invading Russia.

Recording and understanding the rules of bodies in motion was the province of conquerors. Armed with that knowledge and an accurate map, one was certainly well armed for a long campaign.

---

[15] For an extended discussion of the role of wounding in war see Elaine Scarry's *The Body in Pain: The Making and Unmaking of the World* (New York: Oxford UP, 1985).

War games (or strategy games) are derivations, or reductions, of the rules of the physical world. They are, in a word, simulations that are more or less exact but never exactly the same as war itself. In the type of war game I was familiar with in the U.S. Army, the troops would head into the field, be split up into "sides," take up positions and fight one another as if it were "for real." There were, however, lots and lots of rules. As we could not really shoot or kill one another, various devices were utilized to decide what was a "casualty" or a "kill." Nowadays, the military uses laser technology that attaches right onto the muzzle of the weapons, and as the soldier fires blank rounds for real sound effects, the laser fires bursts. This is not exactly the same as firing a real round, for ballistics plays no part in a hit as lasers tend to beam in a straight line and bullets (and especially tumbling rounds like the old M16s fired) are subject to wind and diminishing speed over distance. It is also impractical to "bounce" a laser off the ground as one can with a bullet and, in any case, the soldier on the receiving end of the shot does not have laser sensors all over their body, but in strategic locations such as the head, back, and chest. In a real battle a soldier hit in the leg is just as surely wounded as one hit in the head or chest, though they may still be able to fire weapon for a while longer.

In the older days, troops in training would move into position and either "spar" with blunted weapons or battles would be resolved with some system involving random number generators like dice. In every case, this form of training, like all training for battle, is a type of simulation intended to prepare soldiers of all ranks for performing their assigned tasks under fire. It is not difficult to imagine the generals moving counters about on a real map to "see" where their troops are at any given moment. Forward observers and runners (or radios) are used to get a more or less accurate position on the unit(s) in question and then mark their location on a large-scale map that seems the defining feature of any "headquarters."

Maps, counters, and rules: these are the essential elements of any strategy "game." Those same generals can play out scenarios on their maps with those same counters regardless of whether or not the soldiers are in the field or not. This "budget" version has the advantage of allowing the general to work through problems of terrain and troop strength without actually making the soldiers run about in the muck.

What we now refer to as the "board game" is simply a simplified version of the war simulation game. Not all of these games have "war" as their theme, but the basic principle is the same—all of these games are designed to compete and to win and many of the most popular games (checkers and chess for example) are still clearly tied to their military roots. The greatest generals, I am told, still play chess. What does one "learn" from playing a game like chess?: the player learns how to think in terms of bodies moving in space and time and the inevitable rules of the body that define that movement.

One element of play that board games—be it backgammon or chess or *The Game of Life*—do not strongly emphasize is the element of the role the player takes. All players in a game have a more or less obvious role to play. In chess, as in most strategy games, the players are implicitly Kings or Generals. In *The Game of Life* you play some possible future self, or possible past-self if you are my age. But on type of game in particular began to put an emphasis on the role, or the simulation of the psychology of another person, and that was the historical, miniatures, war game. In *The Game of Life*, for example, you can be, or play like, simply yourself. There is no rule that suggests that you ought to try and behave like someone other than yourself. But like Cowboys and Indians, a type of play which requires that the participants adopt a role based on their knowledge (however stereotypical and incomplete) of the American West, historical miniature war gaming required the participants to try to think like historical military figures and act appropriately. Replaying historical battles became a method for analyzing the strategies and the very minds of long dead military leaders and the participants could ostensibly become like those leaders, at least during the game itself, by engaging in similar, simulated, rule-based, situations. Predictably, miniature, historical war gaming developed as a military instructional tool. It would be, after all, a short step from a miniature based battle map of a current or simulated battle to a recreation of a past battle. But what happens with the historical battle is the necessity to extrapolate the logistics of a previous time. How far the older cannon could shoot, for example, and how likely they were to fail? How much damage could a knights armor take? And, thus, the rule systems became increasingly complex. As those studying historical battles continued to worry over rule systems that would more accurately model the movements of troops, they also began to model the psychology of groups—how likely was one particular unit to surrender and why?

Finally, the minutiae of the rule systems as the rules defining the simulated world, got closer and closer to the individual soldier on the battlefield—how fast could he move, how much could he carry, how much food and water would he need, how much damage could his sword take—the closer we came to numerically defining and simulating, not military units or groups, but individuals caught in the heat of battle. And then there was *Dungeons & Dragons*.

Six: The Measure of Man

I started playing *Dungeons & Dragons* when I was fourteen years old. My father was publisher of the newspaper in Stuttgart, Arkansas: a town best known for rice farming, the World Championship Duck-calling Contest, and the ever popular Mosquito Festival and Duck Gumbo Cook-off. We made one of our monthly runs to the big-city of Little Rock (the only state capitol you can say while clearing your throat, according to my great-grandfather) and, somewhere between hot pretzels and paper cups of Orange Julius, I went to the toy store to buy a new model rocket and walked out with *Dungeons & Dragons* instead. I really had no idea what I had in my hand,s nor how many years later I would still be thinking about that one moment in an otherwise fading past.

Why *Dungeons & Dragons*? Quite simply, it was on the shelf just to the left of the rockets. Which is not to mention the fact that Spielberg's 1982 blockbuster *E.T.: The Extraterrestrial* which featured—among myriad other advertisements, including the once infamous M&Ms vs. Reeses Pieces war—a raucous game of *D&D* in the opening scenes and that was the movie I had just seen. (I am convinced cultural critics now grossly underestimate the actual long-term impact of both Spielberg and Lucas's films and merchandising tactics on American Society. That *D&D*, Reeses Pieces, and Drew Barrymore entered the American Mainstream in the same film should not go unnoted (though what, exactly, that means I will leave to another book).

On the box, I saw an armored man with a sword and a really pissed-off looking red dragon clearly about to bite his head off. That image evoked one of my favorite memories from any book ever: the moment when Bilbo Baggins faces the dragon in J.R.R. Tolkien's *The Hobbit*. That painting told me all I needed to know about the game—somewhere inside of that box was an experience I had always wanted. The box rattled when I shook it. I looked more closely at the cover. *Dungeons & Dragons Fantasy Role-playing Game: Set I: Basic Rules*. And, farther down: "This game requires no game board because the action takes place in the player's imagination with dungeon adventures that include monsters, treasures, and magic. Ideal for 3 or more beginning to intermediate players, ages 10 and up."

I never built or flew another model rocket, and I suppose that may have been the moment when my future career in the aerospace industry came crashing to a halt. There was just something about that sexy red box: something about it gave me chills in a way I still associated with transgression. But this was no weathered copy of *Playboy* furtively hidden in a secret place in my closet, nor the .22 rifle I was never supposed to handle without my father, nor even my canary yellow Suzuki 250 motorcycle that gave me that gut-wrenching sense of freedom. No, this was just a game in a red box that rattled a bit when I shook it; but it promised dragons and treasure and magic, and that was enough. I believe it cost around twenty dollars: one fifth of my monthly take from a small paper-route.

D&D was, in fact, a game you could play without a board. The whole "game" was just a bunch of rules about how things in the fantasy world worked, what types of people there were, what occupations you could be, and what types of ugly (and not so ugly) monsters you were likely to encounter and how likely they were to beat you into a tiny pulp and eat you. The only way to "win" per se was *to survive*. Though *D&D* was at that time easily the most complex game ever offered for "ages 10 and up," at the same time it cut right back to the core of what gaming was really about under all the *Candyland* and *Chutes and Ladders* skins—trying to survive by wits and steel alone. Oh, and magic is good too.

I spent hours upon house pouring over the rules and creating test characters and having them fight monsters from the list of possible terrors. I created elves, dwarves, magic-users, fighters, and thieves. Part of the magic of the game was this engagement with a multi-player game even when alone. The appeal is obvious enough—though it originated with figurine-based battle systems, *D&D* (as it is still affectionately called) draws heavily from mythology and the fantasy world of J. R. R. Tolkien and thereby accessed the lively following of fantasy literature. But, perhaps even more important, it created a malleable context—a virtual world of the imagination—that invited the entrance of the player. The rulebooks themselves belied the emphasis on world-creation with their myth-building and encyclopedic tone of certainty. The rulebooks were not describing a game as much as they were describing a *world*. For example, I still remember the first time I read this entry:

> Elves are slender, graceful demi-humans with delicate features and slightly pointed ears. They are 5 to 5 ½ feet tall and weigh about 120 pounds. They can be dangerous opponents, able to fight with any weapon and use magic spells as well, but prefer to spend their time feasting and frolicking in wooded glades. They rarely visit the cities of men. Elves are fascinated by magic and never grow tired of collecting spells and magic items, especially if the items are beautifully crafted.[16]

Even more specifically were the charts and graphs that offered up Elves in numerical form. These were not simply a mysterious magical creature that appears just in time to save Bilbo from harm but objectively measured and encyclopedically described. I did not need to imagine what an elf could do, I could see it for myself and test it out with a few die rolls. Could an elf beat a dwarf in combat? With the right smarts and some luck in the die rolls, he sure could! It occurs to me now that the creature descriptions really operated like character sketches that a novelist or dramatist might use in preparation for their tale. Here is an example of one that fascinated me when I first read it:

> Carrion Crawler: This scavenger is worm shaped, 9' long and 3' high with many legs. It can move equally well on a floor, wall, or ceiling like a spider. Its mouth is surrounded by 8 tentacles, each 2' long, which can paralyze on a successful hit unless a saving throw [die roll] vs. Paralysis [the minimum chance to avoid the effect] is made. Once

---

[16] *Dungeons & Dragons Fantasy Adventure Game Basic Rulebook*, 1981. B9.

paralyzed, a victim will be eaten (unless the carrion crawler is being attacked). The paralysis can be removed by a cure light wounds spell, but any spell so used will have no other effect. Without a spell, the paralysis will wear off in 2-8 turns.[17]

Though the description certainly has the encyclopedic feel (as no doubt intended) the text also embeds formulas for resolving encounters: if paralyzed the victim will be eaten unless the carrion crawler is being attacked by someone else. Not only does the entry for carrion crawler describe the creature and define its behavior—as any encyclopedia definition for an animal would—it delineates behavior as flatly quantifiable within certain limits which are defined by chance (die rolls).

The back cover of the 1980 Basic Rulebook asserts that "*Dungeons & Dragons* fantasy game is a step out of the ordinary. Each adventure is like writing a novel from a massive set of character analyses. Players assume the roles of Elves, Dwarves, Halflings, or Humans and travel through a fantastic world filled with danger and excitement. Adventurers will wander through frightening dungeons conquering evil foes and meeting terrible dragons."[18] The reference to the novel here is not simply back-cover hype: the idea of a game with an evolving, complex narrative that could equal the narrative enjoyment of the novel—and the world-dissolving immersion effect of a good read—that could also be "entered into" and affected by the "audience" is exactly what Gary Gygax and company envisioned. That *D&D* was very much like a novel is evidenced in the sheer amount of fan-fiction and commercial printed novels that arose from the game, of which the still immensely popular *Forgotten Realms* fantasy novel series is a significant example. That a film by the same name (*Dungeons & Dragons: The Movie*, 2000) hit the screens more than three decades after the first *D&D* wave, and the internet space Facebook had a popular *D&D* plug-in game, belie the staying power of this

---

[17] *Dungeons & Dragons Fantasy Adventure Game Basic Rulebook*, 1981. B32.
[18] *Dungeons & Dragons Fantasy Adventure Game Basic Rulebook*, 1981.

particular role-playing game, at least in the minds of the first generation of players who grew up playing *D&D* and were, in 2013, solidly in their 30's, 40's and beyond. And what all of these players have enjoyed over the last thirty years is what Lawrence Schick, in his book *Heroic Worlds: A History and Guide to Role -Playing Games*, defines as "quantified interactive storytelling."[19] I will discuss this definition in a slightly different order than presented by Schick.

Storytelling—essential to all RPGs is the narrative function of these games. Unlike the usual card game or board game, RPG's are based upon a narrative including setting, characterization, and plot that serves as the very core of the game. Unlike traditional narrative, however, RPGs allow for the characters themselves to choose their path through the settings or series of settings. In a word, the characters come alive in a way not allowed by fiction. The narrative is not driven by a set series of events; rather, the "game" is a series of potentialities as imagined by the game designers and game master (or GM, or DM for dungeon master). The game designers and GM set the stage, so to speak, for the players to act upon. This stage setting usually includes a history of its own, but the players themselves, beginning from this history, engage the narrative through their in-game actions and, therefore, the story will never be the exactly same for different sets of players. An interesting result of this level of narrative choice is that often a great majority of the created setting is never encountered by any one set of players unless the adventure is very brief or the GM is mercilessly domineering (in effect forcing the players into every created situation). What might we think of these "lost narratives"? The parallel in real life would be somewhat equivalent to Schrödinger's Cat Paradox of the unopened box except for the fact that the box has been "opened" so to speak by its creator or the GM. but this is not always the case as many of the outcomes in a game (what might properly be called an "adventure") are determined by randomness, a point we will return to in a moment.

---

[19] Schick 10; Schick attributes Darwin Bromley as the source of the definition

As the players participate in the creation of what will be the local version of the narrative, the RPG is also highly interactive. By way of comparison, we might again return to the novel and consider how Saussure describes the relationship between a word and its referent. Whereas a speaker, even in everyday conversation, receives feedback in terms of verbal replies and body language, the author has a much more limited engagement with the audience through the text. The author has an idea, writes it in language into the text and then the reader interacts with the text (reads it) and receives the information there encoded. But, this is an imperfect process and, as Reader Response theory has taught us, the reader brings a whole life of experiences to the text through which they interpret the encoded information. In essence, now two readers read exactly the same novel though they interested with the same text (words). Thus, there is interaction with the text on the part of the reader. The words do not change, per se, but their meaning does depending on who is doing the reading. One need spend no more than a few minutes in a literature course to see this principle in action.

I once had a student from an urban center read Charlotte Perkins Gilman's short story "The Yellow Wallpaper" as a story about a woman who had been kidnapped and drugged by a gang/cult who was holding her for ransom. He wrote a quite elegant paper explaining his theory to the rest of the class. Following the New Critics, Robert Penn Warren and Cleanth Brooks being chief among them, I often used to refer to these diverse readings as "strong" or "weak" depending on how much direct evidence could be found in the text, but I now refer to them as falling on a scale of "local," "collective," or "global" where a "local" reading exists only in my own mind and is framed entirely by my own experiences, a "collective" reading is shared by a specific cultural group (such as persons from a particular ethnic background or theoretical perspective) and a "global" reading being one that is accepted by the great majority of readers, though complete consensus would never be possible, for as we have already discussed, no two readers read the same text exactly the same way.

Though some theorists have imagined an "Ideal Reader" as the imagined target of the reading as being the reader who could read a text "perfectly" as intended by the New Critics—often perceived as espousing an "ideal reading"—were the first to point out that even the author cannot perfectly understand what they intended or what they have accomplished, what is commonly known as the "intentional fallacy." Freud actually settled that matter for us with his elucidation of the unconscious, though he was by no means the first to point out that we cannot know our whole minds. So, we can safely say that there is quite a bit of interaction between a reader and a written text as the words take shape in the reader's mind. The words themselves may not change, but the fact that no two readers read alike sets a boundary, if you will, on interpretation (see, for example Umberto Eco's *The Limits of Interpretation*), so effectively, there is no "real" text and no "real" monolithic reading of the text. some readings, however, are what we might call "viral" in that they move from local reading to what approaches a global reading and this is the activity that literary critics are engaged in— spreading their reading to the masses in the hopes that it catches on and "takes over" alternate local or collective readings and some of these readings are particularly virulent particularly if the target readers have yet to formulate their own local reading. Particular readings of the Bible, for example, have subsumed large groups of people to their will.

With the invention of RPGs, however, narrative takes a new turn that "opens up" the linguistic triangle so that the narrative comes to be created through a collective process between the game designers, the adventure designer, the GM, and the players. And while it may seem that the level of interaction between the game designers and the players is analogous to the interaction between an author and a reader, this is not the case as games are designed and modified during "play tests" and are further modified based on the input of actual players. Thus RPGs like any game develop over time and the player, unlike the reader, has real potential access to the authors. thus, we see the development from the prototype *Chainmail* to *Dungeons & Dragons* to the *Advanced Dungeons & Dragons* and so on. Even on the local level, around the kitchen table, the rules of the world are often changed by the GM and these changes are encouraged by the designers themselves.[20] Rather than a triangle of fading influence between writer, text, and reader (for the author surely does imagine some sort of audience) the RPG forms a network of influence.

Back at the kitchen table again, the players make choices that add to the setting in order to create the narrative. The story, as such, thus becomes a collective, shared experience of history making, though this history is what we might term "imaginary" or "fictional". But, is it? I was there. I sat at the table. "I" (my character) did things which I recollect having done. The primary difference in this case between traditional narratives like an Epic, for example, is not the collective nature per se—all cultures have myths that they collectively partake in and "remember"—but the collective participation of several subjects (several persons) in a narrative where each of us may say "I remember when we killed that Ogre with an old shoe" or what have you. This is shared experience of a level approaching everyday lived experience. RPGs thus combine the functions and methods of narrative with Mr. Roger's-style make believe.

The other element of RPGs that opens the narrative is the fact that they are quantified. Like the board game or the war game, though to a much greater degree, RPGs attempt to rule the world in the sense that they take actions, and in some cases even personalities, and try to quantify them in some meaningful way. RPGs are based in a quantified "world" which essentially means that the designers of the games decide that certain things are or are not possible. If something *is* possible then it is quantified to a greater or lesser degree. Obviously not all eventualities can be directly quantified; however, eventualities (actions) can be quantified under broader schemes of "physical acts," "mental acts,"

---

[20] An early derivative of D&D, *Tunnels and Trolls*, operates on the looser principle of negotiation. With a very limited set of rules, T&T invites the GM and players to decide what is reasonable in most cases when checking a skill and etc.

and so on, with a base chance to perform any reasonable task. Unreasonable tasks can even be categorized under a heading like "acts of god" with an almost impossible chance of succeeding (say rolling a 1 twenty times in a row). Any action or event that is deemed possible has a quantified chance of succeeding or happening.

Almost all of these quantified elements deal (like physics) with bodies moving in space and time. Often these rules—particularly in the more realistic games— are derived from real bodies moving in real spaces. For example, if a character wants to enter a house by breaking down the door, she will have a quantified chance of doing so—say a 3 in 6 chance on the first attempt for a wood door with a normal lock, a 2 in 6 chance if the door is bolted, a 1 in 6 chance of the door is double bolted or barred (having to essentially break the frame), and a 0 in six if the door is bolted and barred. Using some tool like an axe would increase this chance (say, by +3 per attempt).

These quantified actions may be more or less formalized in rule books, but all refer to perceived limits of the actual body: though not necessarily (nor even often) the body of the actual player. I would have great difficulty breaking down any door on my own, though I might have a base chance called "luck" to hit said door in just the right way. However, my character might be much stronger than my body and may have specific training such as one might receive as a police officer, soldier, or burglar that increases the chance of getting through that door. What all these games suggest— what the narratives support—is that the world is quantifiable (down to individual action) even down to the statistical reference we refer to as "chance." Randomness is a quality that suggests the real world experience where I may luck out and break a door and a trained professional could screw-up and on the first try (shouldn't have had that triple burrito for lunch!). For the RPG designer, just like the scientist, the world is based on rules that may be described in quantifiable terms.

Of course an RPG also creates the possibility for fantastic elements to be normalized as well. I cannot pull down a building like Samson, nor can any living human being, but my character might be able to pull down a building if he *was* Samson or just as strong. That's where the term "role" comes in. Who are you (who is your character) in the created quantified world. The body is, in most games, quantified on some combination of physical and mental attributes. A typical breakdown includes, strength, dexterity, intelligence, wisdom, constitution, and charisma. How strong, how fast (or nimble), how smart, wise, and socially attractive is your virtual body? On the typical *AD&D* scale I might rate myself as follows (on a 20 point scale):

Strength   8
Dexterity   12
Intelligence   18
Wisdom   13
Constitution   10
Charisma   15

In real-life (or RL in game speak) we can think of people who represent the maximum in each of these categories. For example we might think of Arnold Schwarzenegger, Harry Houdini, Stephen Hawking, the Dali Lama, 50 cent, Bill Clinton, or Ronald Reagan as having 20s in charisma (though I only voted for one of them). The list reads rather like "On a scale of 1-10 who is the better looking?" and indeed, at the very base it *is* just such a list.

However, there is an additional subjective element: when actually playing a game, you have to take into consideration my RL body (at least the brain portion) as well, because I might think of something, some way out of a situation for example, that my character would never be smart enough to do. Or, a particularly dense player might have a character that is much smarter than his real life counterpart. The character *should* know how to solve a puzzle, but the real life player just can't quite seem to figure it out. This is where the Game Master comes into play as she takes this imbalance into account by indicating to the player that the character has no chance of doing something even though the player can think of it, or by suggesting to the dense player that they might try a particular tactic or have just had a flash of insight. These conversations are invariable carried out with the second person, "You have an idea," and not the third person, "Your character has an idea." This intrusion of the GM into the collective, complex real-life/virtual self (collectively called the "player character" or PC) creates an active rupture in typical notions of the "self."

This negotiation between RL player, the character, the made world, and the GM creates a vital space for role-playing and provides a window into the world of the self. It can also lead to some rather humorous events. I was once with a party that spent twenty minutes of real time examining what eventually turned out to be an imaginary piece of broken glass. Our characters were very strong and powerful but not particularly bright, and the GM led us on for quite a while as we checked the "glittering thing" for magic and tried to estimate the value of this "gem-like substance" we found in the road. I still tell this story and it always reminds me that RPGs are both story-based (created with narratives) and are story generators.

RPG's are also story based. The story frame is laid out by the GM (or a professional module or scenario designer) and the PCs negotiate the terrain making their own choices within those rules and thereby creating, in complex with the GM, their own story. Again, the RPG suggests that lived experience is a negotiation between the PC (the collective "I") the quantified world, and the GM (everyone else and the Gods) who becomes the voice of the world. The body is turned into words. The world is turned into words. "I am going to kick the wall" "You are kicking the wall." What happens?" "Your toe hurts. You think it might be broken."

The GM thus serves as my nervous system in the game relaying back to me what my body is experiencing. Summarized briefly, the experience of single player in an RPG might sound something like this: 1) There are things I can do and things I cannot; 2) of the things I can do, there is always a percent chance to do so; 3) I (the player) may think I can do things I cannot; 4) I may think or do things I never thought of or could do; 5) I may do things I do not want to do; 6) I may not know things I know (such as the laws of electricity or how to type); 7) I may know things I do not (magic for example); 8) I require an outside negotiator to communicate with my complex body. Though RPGs are, at the end of the day, *games*, the potential for redefining the way we think about ourselves as individual subjects is very great and has not, I believe, been adequately explored. I have actually seen avid RPG players roll dice "to hit" for everyday activities such as asking a girl to dance. Though this is a bit of a joke, they roll the dice nevertheless. Is deciding whether or not to dance with someone random? Does it have a random element? What does this type of thinking say about the guy who wants to ask a girl to dance? Regardless, something has shifted in the ways we can see the world and one option has become to see the world a complex quantifiable system with a core element of luck. Even more—the world, right down to individual performance, can be *simulated*.

RPGs thus represent the next evolutionary jump in virtuality following art, cartography, and narrative. I believe RPGs were perceived as being so "addictive" (an abused term if there ever was one) because virtuality is an essential part of what it means to be human. In a certain sense RPGs are more real than real life because they replicate the interior feelings we all have that narratives should be true, that we all have multiple selves, that imagination and dream have their own reality, and that the world has rules (that we cannot fully know in real life). By playing an RPG, we engage with others on a deeper level of consciousness where we admit in the act of playing that reality itself seems "unreal," which is itself a feeling, psychoanalytic theorist Jaques Lacan would tell us, that comes from the process of individuation. In playing an RPG, in the act of playing a character, we admit the unsatisfactory performative nature of our own lives and thoroughly enjoy the admission. There is pleasure in performance of all types but the RPG, like acting in a drama, is a collective creation of a virtual reality, a "making real" of the imaginary which is actually a "making real" of that other psychic reality that lies buried within all of us.

Seven: Life on the Screen

The cultural terrain of Generation X was defined by George Lucas, Stephen Spielberg, videogames, and MTV.[21] On the silver screen films like *Jaws* (1975), *Star Wars* (1977), and *Close Encounters of the Third Kind* (1977), and *Indiana Jones: Raiders of the Lost Ark* (1981) were drawing crowds to the theater in record numbers and for the first time in history film merchandising produced more revenue than the films themselves, despite the fact that many movie-goers saw these films, *Star Wars* in particular, over and over again. Back in the house, MTV (first airing in 1981) was the television show that launched thousands of careers for the likes of Madonna, Cindy Lauper, The Cars, Fresh Prince, and Run DMC. In 1972, Atari's *Pong* gave birth to the video arcade where millions of teenagers spent trillions of quarters playing games like *Space Invaders* (1978), *Galaxian* (1979), *Centipede* (1981), and, of course, the inimitable *Pac-man* (1980) and it's even more popular sequel, *Ms. Pac-man* (1981). Then, the release of Atari's *Pong* home console in 1975 ensured that a whole generation would be glued to the television like never before.

Both television and film combine the narrative elements of myth and fiction with the visual element of the arts. On the screen, myths come alive and our imagination, our greatest hopes and deepest fears, take shape. It should come as no surprise, then, that of the earliest themes in cinema, science fiction, the fantastic, and horror predominate and many of these focus on the creation of virtual beings. As I will discuss later, part of the subversive nature of virtual environments is located in the virtual body, or the avatar. As we are aware from cyberpunk fiction, the very notion of a virtual body had a profound impact on the subject matter of television and film. From the fiction of William Gibson to *Star Trek: The Next*

---

[21] Atari's *Pong* was not the first commercial home video game system. Magnavox's Odyssey released in 1972 holds that title; but the success of *Pong* started the home videogame sensation and launched an industry still vibrant to this day.

Generation and *The Matrix*, the idea of vitality has permeated our society and become a very synecdoche for postmodernism itself.

Stating the obvious—or, what we might rather call, "the readily apparent to anyone not crazy or a fool"—has increasingly become a lost art in academe and it distances the academic writer, often unnecessarily, from the broader audience. Thus, I would like to begin this discussion of film with a statement of what many of you will see as the "obvious" characteristics of cinematic representations of the virtual in cinema. Let's begin with the word "virtual" itself. The etymology of the word—and perhaps I should note that it is an adjective, though we most often mistakenly use it as a noun these days as I just did above—is from the Latin *ob* (against) and *via* (way). The *obvious* is that which literally stands in your way. You either see it or you will bump into it. That is fine and dandy when it comes to a five-foot wide pothole in the road or an angry bear on your car hood, but where the physically obvious can often be agreed upon, the figuratively obvious often cannot be agreed upon and often is culturally defined. The moon obviously circles the earth only because we are now taught to see it that way. Most people do not give it much thought, just as most people did not give much thought to the obvious fact that the sun circled the earth for most of human history. The obvious not only means *in plain sight* but also an *obstruction* and an obstruction is something that must be dealt with or we endanger our ability to move forward.

I will, therefore, start by stating that the impulse behind the creation of cinema is desire: the desire to communicate, to tell a good story, the desire to represent new and interesting worlds, and in the case of much film, the desire to make money. These are just a few of the possible desires which give rise to the cinematic art form and they are not particular to it. There are also desires expressed in the film and cinematic technique as well. Most notable of these is the desire to see. All told, the human is a highly voyeuristic animal and we like to watch. Watching gives us pleasure. Current medical wisdom suggest that the male of the species is more visually oriented than the female who seems to prefer narrative, but this strikes me as a cultural phenomenon and not a biological one, and the argument tends to come up most often in the discussion of pornography: men prefer, it is said, visual pornography and women prefer narrative pornography (erotic literature). What all these arguments are really saying is simply "men like to look and women like to listen" but this has surely not always been true, and since both image and words are attempts to communicate, both are sign systems and they have the same root. The supposed male preference for the visual is, I believe, a local cultural phenomenon that becomes inscribed on our biology: hard-wired after birth and not before. In any case, both men and women certainly enjoy watching cinema—all discussion of "chick flicks" aside. We will bypass for now the outer versus inner nature of the male and female. Men and women certainly have different anatomies, but even the brute fact of the penis and vagina are wrapped in layers upon layers of history.

Though I am not an Aristotelian in all cases, Aristotle's defense of the arts as bringing about a catharsis in the receiver still applies today. We make what we fear either in its positive or negative aspect: which is to say we make horror movies not because we want or like to be afraid but because we *are* afraid, and watching them allows the release of that fear. We make love stories because we are afraid that we will be alone, that we are alone, and because, ultimately, we are afraid that we will die. Death has always been the source of greatest fear for humans and therefore much of our artistic expression (including mythology and religion) has focused on death. Comedies make us forget that we will die (or laugh at death). Tragedies allow us to virtually lose loved ones and, to die vicariously.

Television and cinema are no different. What they shows us is what we have inside, and mostly all of that is based in the fear of death as Freud, Jung, Lacan, and many others have variously argued. The particulars are less important here than the obvious. We are all afraid of death and we all live mourning our own inevitable death. Thus the attraction of narrative and myth from the beginning—stories have the power to immortalize and many stories tell us that there is another life after this one. The performance in theater, the creation of a character, the choice of an actor, costuming, and setting all vie towards the creation of a person and place that do not, or no longer, exist. The body of the actor fills a form, wrapping about themselves an avatar night after night. They walk in another's shoes. Who can we say makes this thing we call a "character" in a play, in a film, or on television? Can one person be said to be responsible for the complex activity of bringing to virtual life a virtual being? Where does the character come from when the performance begins? Where does she go when the performance ends?

Transferring the same notion to film: In *Romeo + Juliet*, which I sometimes use in my class on Love and Death, I watch Juliet dance with Paris as Romeo looks on and her face is the actress Claire Danes' with those large eyes and that signature dimpled smile. The scene as we see it, the place that this "Juliet" lives, was created by a writer and realized by a director operating under the direction of a set of producers who in turn operate under a studio in the Hollywood system. I ask again, where does "Juliet," this "Juliet," come from? Who is she? What is she? Shakespeare wrote the play between 1591 and 1595 (and it was most likely performed then as well) and it was first published in 1597. Is this the same Juliet?

They say that actors and directors bring characters to life but I think, rather, that they simply create the context for an already living thing to manifest. The psychiatrist Carl Gustav Jung would term this process embodying an archetype and in that sense the performance is not unlike the physical manifestations of the gods in mythology. Those human forms, of course, are referred to as avatars, and this is the origin of our contemporary use of the word. The actress Claire Danes embodies the archetype of Juliet and, for a short while, becomes her, but she does not "give Juliet life" as we like to say, for the character has a life of its own. The story has a life of its own and we can see the story physically manifested on the stage or on television or on film. But as any Media Studies expert— or actor, or writer, or director—could tell you: these three mediums are not identical. I would like to discuss the primary differences between theater and film and television as questions of *immediacy*, *interaction*, and *immersion*.

The brute physicality of live actors in front of a live audience adds an *immediacy* to the unfolding story that lends credibility to it. Even if the story is an ancient one of Clytemnestra's killing of her husband Agamemnon or of Odysseus gouging out his own eyes, the audience sees it happening here (on the stage) and now—what we now like to term a "live audience" which, again, is rather like saying "real milk from real cows". Furthermore, even the most flaccid audience has an impact on the actors on the stage and vice versa, what I am calling here *interaction*. The history of theater is filled with both intentional and unintentional audience interactions and from all accounts early theater was a highly participatory affair as audiences cheered for heroes, shouted down the villains, threw rotten fruit, and etc. In theater, the immediacy and interaction, if properly maintained, lead to *immersion*, or the sense that what one is seeing is real. In one well-documented case, a performance of Shakespeare's *Othello* was interrupted by a man who leapt from the audience onto the stage and stabbed the play's villain, Iago, to death. This was certainly much more *interaction*, *immediacy*, and (excuse the inevitable pun) *immersion* than the actor playing Iago would have wanted, but it serves to underscore the point that audiences can become so immersed in a tale as to mistake it for actual reality.

Cinema, however, removed the audience from the time and place of the action (as the phonograph and radio had previously distanced the voice) and distanced the bodies of the actors from those of the audiences. In New York, for example, early films were often run in one of the many burlesque houses where the silver screen literally replaced the bodies of the performers on the stage. In fact, the term "grind house," which is sometimes used for a cheap movie theater or adult video store, originates from the "bump and grind" dance of the female dancers in burlesque.

After film took the actors off the stage to be replaced by a screen, television did away with the theater all together. The occasional resurgence of popularity in "live" television programming (such as with *Saturday Night Live*) harks back to the desire of the television audience sitting at home to experience some of the immediacy and engagement of live theater, without, of course, the bother of actually going to a theater and sitting with a large group of people for a few hours. But even this sort of programming is one-way, which is why many "live shows" also have a "live audience" to simulate the effect of theater even though in the studio the actors and crew make little attempt to pretend that a television show is being broadcast and filmed as they pause for commercial breaks, change sets in front of the audience, and etc. Ultimately, the production is not for the studio audience at all; the members of the studio audience are, rather, part of the production itself. People are brought in (and sometimes pay for the privilege) to play the part of the audience. They become, for the space of the show, actors in bit parts of audience members who rehearse their parts (albeit briefly) and are coached in their responses with cue-cards and etc.

Videogames re-instated the audience (the player) as a participatory element in the drama on the screen by drawing from the immediacy and interaction of the theater to induce immersion, though they do so within the context of film and television. While RPGs opened narrative structures to broaden the base of the virtual space and emulated real-life experiences in a way that was previously not possible, the invention of the video game gave us an interactive visualization of virtual space itself creating, in effect, a digitized "text" that could be perceived as a "space," and "virtual reality" came into the living room for the first time. And, looking back to the halcyon days of my early teen years, I have to wonder: what was the deal was with *Pong*? I mean, really. With the perfect vision of hindsight, perhaps the strangest thing about video games is that we played *Pong* at all. Yet, *Pong*, with its chunky wood veneer case and wheels to move the "paddles" up and down the screen in pursuit of the little, light "ball" set the stage for uncountable hours of game play and, now, a whole generation brought up on videogames. What was it about the early videogames that spawned an industry? How did *Pong* become the game that launched a thousand videogame consoles?

I can clearly remember the novelty of being able to "watch television" and "play a game" at the same time, which combined two of my favorite pastimes. In the 1970's "playing a game" had become an activity specifically targeted to getting the kids, or even the whole family, away from the boob-tube. *Pong* ended all that: suddenly the whole family could sit in front of the television and interact by playing a game on the screen. However, the real power of *Pong*, the real source of the joy of playing it, was interacting with the TV and actually making something happen "in there". Let's face it, you can yell at the television all day long (as my great-grandfather often did) and nothing is going to happen in, or on, the screen as a result. Television, even more so than written narrative, is a passive medium supplying both the narrative and the images for the viewer. The main interaction between the viewer and the modes of television production come from the cultural base—we belong to the same culture—and feedback through letters and generalizing show ratings. *Pong* gave us a chance to make the TV console do something and, thereby, in a pathetic sort of way we could all be "on TV" and "in there."

The desire to be "on TV" is, essentially, the desire to be famous and achieve recognition just like one might desire to be a ballerina, singer, actor, or anyone famous and recognized by others. But television is most closely akin to the various forms of theater because of the similarity between the stage and the frame of the television set. This similarity transfers into a feeling that the television screen actually incorporates space through the flat screen. We say that someone is "on television" in the same way we say that someone is "on stage"—not on a flat surface, but occupying a certain created three-dimensional space. Understandably, the conventions of speech surrounding the television mirror those of drama just as drama mirrors the plastic arts where the stage creates a scene surrounded the frame of the stage. A drama is a painting plus narrative incorporating representations of bodies, space, and time. The television adds to the dimensions of body, space, narrative, and time the element of distance. We do not need to go to the theater to see the show on TV. With pre-recorded programming, TV further incorporated the non-sequential nature of recorded music. Cinema had first combined recorded music with moving images, but one still had to go somewhere, into a theater, to see one. Thus, the videogame is the culmination of a variety of processes including the representation of body, space, narrative time, sound, a quantified world, and (albeit severely limited at first) a sense of immediacy (the sense that "something is really in there" as opposed to "at the studio), and of interaction (the ability to make things happen), all of which enabled the strongest conglomeration of immersive technologies and techniques ever assembled. It was not very long before video games began to experiment with different points-of-view, arguably the most immersive of which is the three-dimensional (3D), first-person point-of-view. The first three-dimensional (3D) game with a first-person point-of-view I remember playing was in a video arcade that occupied a mobile building, one of those mobile home units modified for construction-site offices and such, set-up in the gravel parking lot of our local bicycle and motorcycle shop. Selling new and used bicycles, motorcycles (everything from mini dirt-bikes on up massive trikes), and parts, the guy must have been doing pretty well already when he got the idea to set up an arcade with a large number of videogames. Before I saw that arcade, the only videogames I had seen were in bars that occasionally passed for restaurants so the drinkers could bring their kids. The videogames were clearly intended for the adults as they were too tall for most kids and no step-stools were provided. At these late night 1970's gatherings us kids usually ended up sitting under the table and playing go-fish while the adults talked about adult things with the jukebox blaring country music. We could occasionally hear the faint "bleep-bloop" of *Space Invaders* in the background.

The video arcade, on the other hand, provided step-stools for all the games and the 3D game I played was *Red Baron*. Red Baron was an elementary flight simulator-type game with line-drawn pyramidal mountains and opponent planes that you were supposed to shoot down. The perspective was first person as if sitting in the cockpit of a biplane, though none of the plane itself could be seen.

The "bullets" were bits of light (pixels) that shot from the sides of the screen thus creating the illusion of actually sitting in a plane and flying above a somewhat detailed plain. This initial foray into popular 3D play heralded the coming of progressively more detailed 3D, first-person perspective available in game worlds such as *Half-Life, EverQuest* and *World of Warcraft*.

The birth of the video role-playing game (VRPG) gave the player of traditional pencil-and-paper role-playing game (RPG) something to do between "real" games, though it also quickly served as a sort of advertising for RPGs in general and VRPGs soon became a phenomenon in and of itself. In the arcades Cinematronic's animated *Dragon's Lair* (1983), a fantasy-adventure movie-style RPG with animations by a former Disney animator Don Bluth, invited players to become Dirk the Daring and attempt rescue Princess Daphne from the evil dragon Singe. At home on the Atari 2600, *Adventure* (1979, developed from a text-based game designed by William Crowther in the mid 1970's), with its little red square for a "hero," may have seemed paltry and infantile compared to the *Dragon's Lair*, but the storyline was much more complex and players had a broader range of choice which added to the "interactive narrative" feel of the game. *Adventure* served as the template for games like the massively popular *Zelda* series, launched with *The Legend of Zelda* for the Nintendo game system in 1987 and still played today. Another example, now billionaire Richard Garriott's long running *Ultima* series (released in 1980 with *Ultima I*) helped launch the online gaming craze with *Ultima Online* (launched 1997) that continues to grow to this day. But, more of that later.

When my family moved away from my original D&D group, I found great solace in playing D&D-based games like *Adventure* on the console and *Might and Magic* on my first PC. They allowed me an outlet for my personal fantasy life of swords and sorcery. The rules were, of course, more restrictive as no computer program as yet can match the imagination and improvisational skills of a real-life GM. The tension of the VG's is more in the numbers than the visuals.

It was also often a lonely affair, though I have seen groups of eight or ten people sitting about a computer screen offering advice and anecdotes while one person plays. I often wondered why they didn't just pull out the manuals and dice and play a real game, but when I asked about this the usual answer was that it simply took too much time. Eight hours later they would all still be sitting there or lying on the bed or floor. I rather think that the activity was enjoyable in an entirely different way from pencil-and-paper games—somewhere between watching a movie with friends and watching a tennis match where one of the people playing is a personal friend. Truly one gets the sense that the computer or program is a person who is out to get you and they, whoever they are, simply must be beat. The space "in there," in the screen, becomes a dangerous and aggressive space packed with aggressive bodies that appear and disappear, live and die, and are reborn none the worse for wear—though often, especially in the early games, the villains are born without the memory of having met you before. All of us VR avatars look alike.

It was inevitable that videogame logic and videogame perspective would leak out into the world at large. I have never played *Frogger*, though I have seen how it works, and yet I still cannot cross a busy New York City street without thinking of the game and both seeing the cars rushing at me in my real-life first person perspective as well as videogame third-person perspective. I suspect that third-person perspective is what really adds to my anxiety. I imagine myself being splatted by an ambulance as if seen from above.

It was also inevitable that the VRPG would incorporate 3D technology, and this inclusion made for the first "realistic" games in that they incorporated the world creating rule systems of RPGs with the growing detail of the VG space. Though the cabinet versions understandably were more detailed and complex, home games (now also PC based) became increasingly popular as players sought to recreate the experience of playing RPGs alone, and now they could see the created world in more detail and from a first person perspective. this change had the effect of putting the player in the game as the protagonist and not simply as the controller of a standardized avatar. The games were still not particularly detailed or complex and often operated, as did early installments of the popular *Might and Magic* series, on a series of still images simulating movement. Eventually these games would come to incorporate real time play as well thus creating the first real-time virtual role-playing worlds. Thus, the elements which would eventually set the VRPG apart from the RPG were the visual representation, solo play, the potential for real-time play all of which added to the player's sense of "immersion" in the game world. Lost, of course, at least at first, was the negotiation between the player, other players, and the GM who controlled the rules of the world. Also gone, in almost all cases, were the world-defining rules themselves as the average player did not have access to an extensive "rule book" like the Dungeon Master's Guide in AD&D and generally had to rely on a limited player manual and experimentation in the game to discover what was possible and what was not. The rules, of course, were intractable and could not be changed except through hacking the game itself or through various other glitches that produced what are now called "exploits."

Thus, the 3D VRPG completed the circle of TV, VGs, and RPGs by creating a visible and audible, interactive virtual world. Of course, there were many virtual environments that were not VRPGs, but only the VRPG approached anywhere near the complexity of RL AND (complexity of narrative) created rules for what the VR body could and could not do in any meaningful way.

VRPGs were certainly not as complex as traditional RPGs, but it would only be a short time before VRPG game design would catch up with the RPG in that department. What the VRPGs really lacked from the RPGs then, was a strong sense of reciprocal interaction, and that interaction would come from the internet. The history of the internet (and Al Gore's participation in it) has been well documented elsewhere, so suffice it to say that the long-term impact of the internet of interest to us here was the advent of interactive, virtual spaces that could host hundreds and even thousands of participants at a time from all over the world.

The progression from email to real-time chat created the virtual space for the text-based games, like *Bedlam* and *Zork*, to become interactive. Now, players could create text personas (more or less detailed text bodies or text-based avatars) that interacted with other text-based avatars in text-based environments. Massive worlds were created and, though not all of these were "games" in the traditional sense all partook of the history of RPGs in defining the limits of their worlds. For the first time virtual bodies were interacting at a distance and the potential for deep role-play became a real possibility. You could be who, or what, you wanted within the framework created by the game designers. Many of these environments had only the barest of available rules (how to talk and move, etc) leaving the player to fend for themselves in the virtual world.

I first played one of these games while a graduate instructor at East Texas State University (now Texas A&M University-Commerce) on the networked computer in my office. The setting of the game was a space station in orbit around earth and the goal of the game (if one choose to "play" at all, as it was possible just to hang out and chat) was to make virtual money, find and decorate an apartment, and live a virtual life online. This was what we would not call a "social" game where the primary purpose was to interact with others. Exploring, making money, and all that served the ultimate goal of player interaction.

Other than the cute acronyms which are strangely reminiscent of the children's toy that went "A cow goes 'moo'" and mud-pies, what could be so appealing about MOOs and MUDs that people would even bother with them? Why not just go to a real location and talk to people physically present? The typical street answer is typically because anyone who spends that much time "alone" at a computer talking to people they have never met face-to-face is some kind of loser-geek. Though, with the advent of popular online social spaces such as MySpace, Facebook, and IMVU and games like *World of Warcraft* that draw a massive audience from the non-gamer population, this perception is changing somewhat. But when the MOOs and MUDs (from here on I will use MUD to represent both) hit the screen, they were all about geekery and still are. And by geekery I mean fantasy, science fiction, horror, and myriad niche interests that swarm around computer and tech culture. The interest of science fiction fans in virtual interactive environments is easy enough to understand—they are looking into the future just as they do when they read. But the stronger impulse for all the groups is the ability to create and participate in interactive environments based on the "worlds" they read about and imagine. No matter the genre or area of interest, the participant in a MUD is helping "write the world" even if in a very small way. In some cases this "writing" is a simple as a character description: "You see before you a very large pink dragon wearing a green wizard's hat that is much too small. The dragon looks you over with her emerald eyes and you get the uncomfortable feeling that she—yes *she!*—is hungry." Or the level of interaction could be as complex as the construction of spaces with complete descriptions within the parameters of the coding of the environment, or even the writing of actual computer code to define what is possible in the "world." There are numerous resources for those interested in how these different levels of interaction work and are accomplished, but what is important here is that MUDs enabled text-based spaces where the participants could interact with one another and the very fabric of the made-world itself. Much like the real world, anything you do, anything you say might have long reaching impact. Through the interaction, the text-based MUDs also created a sense of *immediacy*. In the worlds of MUDs things are happening *now* and if you aren't there, you are missing it, and this immediacy, like a party eternally in progress that you are always missing, is one of the factors that leads to an increased sense of *immersion.*

Another factor in the sense of immersion is that MUDs are essentially performances; or, to be more specific the player-participant engages spontaneous text-based performances. Like impromptu theater where one actor assumes a role, either of their own making or given to them randomly, and then must play that role off of the other actors' performances of their roles. That the same methods (role-play) are often used in psychoanalysis and other forms of psychological treatments is telling—humans have a tendency to see the world in terms of roles and the performance of those roles. Most, if not all, of us are able to "impersonate" other people we know or have seen or heard. We are able to mimic basic personality traits, comportment, signature movements, quirks of speech, and so on. Impersonation is essentially a later form of play that takes the form of mimicry where the child mimics the adult performance of an action or attitude as a type of informal life-training.

MUDs create virtual, text-based environments (or "spaces," though the prolific use of this term has recently come under question) for the performance of roles and allow for experimentation and play with roles in a relatively risk-free environment compared to the potentially dangerous circumstances surrounding real-world experimentation. As a researcher who often writes about gender issues, for example, I am often surprised with by the horrendous acts committed against persons who deviate from what is considered the "norm" of sexual behavior. Films like *Victor, Victoria* (1982) may make light of the persecution of those who live different lifestyles from the run-of-the-mill heterosexual couples, but the danger is real and omnipresent even in liberal communities like those in San Francisco and New York, where hate-crimes against gays, lesbians, transsexuals, and transgender persons (and even for persons who occasionally choose to simply dress in a creative manner) still occur at an astonishing rate.

However, the engagement that results from the freedom to experiment with roles, can also pose psychological dangers. Like the actor who played Iago, the villain of Shakespeare's *Othello*, so convincingly that an audience member stabbed him anger, an online performance can be so convincing that others might feel that they have been lied to, betrayed, or manipulated and, in the worst cases, could suffer real psychological trauma. Examples of these cases abound in the popular press and discussions of the ethics of online performances are becoming increasingly common in academic circles.

On the other side of the screen, the engaged player can become so invested—a stronger form of psychological engagement—in a character that they become increasingly open to psychological effects and even harm. This psychological openness is certainly not unknown outside the internet community. We see examples throughout history and virtually every single day in the newspapers and tabloids of actors of the stage, television, and film who suffer from a variety of psychological issues and who engage in self-destructive behaviors due to their problems of identity. That Heath Ledger (1979-2008), for example, dies of a drug and alcohol overdose at the end of filming *Batman: The Dark Knight* (2008) where he plays a most insane incarnation of the Joker is perhaps circumstantial, but the history of psychological problems in the acting world is not debatable. And the probably causes—low self-esteem, fear of rejection, rapid wealth gain, rapid fame, and so on—can be tied to the overall artificiality of performance as a self-reflexive process. When one performs others as a profession, many of the characters being conjured from the mind of a writer or team of writers—it seems inevitable to me that an actor at some point comes to question whether they have an essential core of self that is "real". In fact, some narratives explore this very theme of the breakdown of reality due to performance beginning as early as Calderon de la Barca's *Life is a Dream* (1635, *La vida es sueño*) where a young prince raised in a tower must come to terms with what he perceives to be the imaginary world outside the tower, Jorge Luis Borges' story "The Circular Ruins" (1940, *"Las ruinas circulars"*) in which a man decides to dream a man into existence only to learn that he himself is a dream, and Miguel de Unamuno's novella *Niebla* (1914) where the protagonist resolves to kill his author and which serves as the basis for the recent film *Stranger than Fiction* (2006) starring Will Farrell. There are many more examples of this type of self-reflexive theater—more than enough, in fact, to support the notion that writers and actors—indeed, anyone in the performance industry—keenly feel the anxiety of performance. Which is not to say the rest of us are not susceptible to "existential angst," but that those classes of persons who job it is to simulate reality, create alternate realities, and even imagine impossible realities, are understandably more prone, in general, to seeing all of reality as "performed," "constructed," or even "fake."

However, as the rest of us increasingly enter into virtual environments and engage in overt performances—as opposed to the usual day-to-day performance as a husband, wife, co-worker, or any of the other roles we generally perform without too much reflection—we become more and more likely to question *all* of our activities as performances so that suddenly I become more often, and more intensely, self-conscious of my role as a "teacher" in the classroom. As in acting, this self-consciousness of the performance can have benefits and drawbacks. By reflecting on my practices in the classroom, for example, I can more astutely alter those practices to be more effect and be *proactive* in my course design and implementation and less *reactive* to incidental events such as tardiness and class outbursts. I can, in effect, check my normal shy, easily hurt, scatter-brained self at the door and "put on" my teacher persona who is much more outgoing, self-confident and organized. I actually do this every day that I teach and reflecting on what works and does not work in the classroom for me and my students has dramatically improved my overall classroom performance and the creation of a culture of learning in the classroom. I perform the best teacher I can be and refine that performance over time. Conversely, however, I have also become more interested in the nature of personality and I could certainly see how such an interest unmediated could turn into a concern or even an unhealthy obsession.

Another factor of the MUD environments that invites a strong engagement or immersion is the logical structure of the made world and this structure has its roots in both games and drama. In both games and drama, the world is reduced or restricted, roles are clearly defined, and the terms of success and failure are clearly defined. Furthermore, the limits of the virtual body—though the performance of that body experiences apparent unrestricted creativity—is likewise clearly defined. In typical drama bodies are defined by an array of artifices including the printed dialog, stage directions, entrance and exit cues, costuming, stage design, the history of performance, and so on. The actor performs within these defined limits and usually does not "do whatever" (though some performances may have the feel of unfortunate spontaneity). In fact, this defining of the bodies on the space of the stage is the meaning of the term *director*. The director is the person charged with directing, or disciplining, the actors' bodies as they perform characters. Likewise, in games like *D&D*, we have a numerical, quantified body engaging with a quantified world mediated by the GM. The same is true in MUDs but to an even greater degree: these computer generated worlds are made entirely of rules written in computer code. They quite literally *are* a set of rules which ultimately are a set of numerical equations. Thus, like the actor and like the player in a game, the participant in a MUD finds comfort in a world of restriction where everything but the individual performance and the interaction with other performances has been clearly defined and mapped out beforehand, and this existential certainty can be immensely comforting.

Unlike our real world experience, defined as it is by the preeminence of modern technology and science where new theories of how the universe work seem to fly daily off the television screen, the online world of MUDs has definite rules: and not only can those rules be learned and understood on many different levels from the rules of game play all the way down to the machine codes, the zeroes and ones, upon which the world is built, not only can they be known but they *are known*. Even as I type "head east" and "open door" and "head west" and thereby navigate through virtual rooms that I have never seen, even as I discover new places and new designs of trees and follow new quests into virtual mountains where virtual monsters try and eat me, even during all of that someone, or a group of someone's, out there, behind the screen, somewhere in the world, knows how and why all this works. And, ultimately, that is a comforting thought for most of us. Suddenly the world is not built on chaos theory, fractals, or string theory, or radical behaviorism, spooky action at a distance, butterfly effect, global warming, solar cooling, or viral memes; or any of the other postmodern sciences and philosophies that increasingly assert that the universe is a damned odd, immensely huge, and disturbingly unpredictable place that is primarily hostile to carbon-based life forms. The universe of this MUD was built by Bob and Jenny and Kim who work in Encino. But, they did not just build a virtual world, they built a philosophy that (however unintentionally) harkens back to the comforting days when everything in the universe seemed known or at least knowable. Whether those in the know were perceived to be gods, philosophers, or diligent scientific researchers, the overall feeling is the same—no matter how screwed up the universe seems right here right now in my living-room, it all makes sense to someone, somewhere.

I have recently been re-reading Charles Darwin's *The Voyage of H.M.S Beagle* (the second edition of 1845),[22] the work preceding *Origin of Species* which describes in chronological order Darwin's almost five years of adventures and discoveries as the Beagle and her crew as they circumnavigate the globe on a survey mission. I was singularly struck by Darwin's irrepressible excitement as he tries to figure out how things work and why and his joy at making what seems a logical connection, of figuring out how something came to be, and solving the geological "puzzle" left before him. I have felt the exact same way as Darwin in two endeavors—one is in researching and writing as I am doing now and the other is when I am playing online games like MUDs and their bigger graphic-based descendent: the massively multi-player role-playing game (MMORPGs which we will discuss somewhat later). I have felt the same wonder and fascination, followed by an intense desire to know what it is all about and how it was all done, how it was made, and what it means. This feeling can transform into the creative impulse—the desire, like the experimental scientist, to replicate what you see and thereby understand it more fully. Computer programmers and engineers often talk lovingly about when they

---

[22] Charles Darwin, *Journal of Researches into the Natural History & Geology of the Countries Visited During the Voyage of the H.M.S. Beagle under the Command of Capt. Fitz Roy, R.N.*

built their first computer or wrote their first computer game. Participants in online environments also participate in the creative process by engaging with the made world and altering it, or adjusting it, with their own interactions. From designing whole buildings using the tools provided by the designers, to simply buying a virtual chair with virtual money—"Congratulations! You have just purchased a plush Victorian chair covered in emerald green satin with gold trim"—and placing that chair in their virtual apartment the player is helping build an individual world that has a personality, character, and feel all its own. And what player hasn't wondered how the heck that chair got from the virtual store to the virtual apartment? How does it know you bought it? How does it know to stay there? What would be philosophical questions in a real living-room become technical questions—the truth is, in fact, out there for any technical minded person who cares to read up on the subject. That certainty is a comforting fact.

But because, as Freud assured us, humans are the neurotic monkeys, anything psychologically comforting also must come with its attendant fear. In pleasure there is always pain. And so we return to cinema—the great purgatory of the American psyche—for some lessons in what scares us about our virtual selves.

Eight: Virtual Fears

Much has been said in the popular press for the last 30 years about the dangers of video games. Role-playing games also came under attack around the same time as being satanic—one of my own *AD&D* books, the *Dungeon Masters' Guide* which featured a large red demon on the cover, was doused in lighter fluid and burned in a rusty 50 gallon drum by a friend's mother when I accidentally left it at his house. She'd read somewhere that *D&D* was a gateway activity to drug use, the ritual killing of small animals, witchcraft, and eternal damnation.

So little evidence exists to support the notion that any of these activities are directly related to (as in a cause of) psychological problems and violent behavior that I am loathe to support such unfounded arguments by examining them here. What I do know— and what all these stories do tell us—is that we, as a culture, fear something about role-playing games, video games, and online culture, among myriad other fears like the impact of violent music and public toilet seats. These fears are certainly aired in the popular press, but the popular press, as flighty and "of the moment" as it has come to be, does not represent the real complexity of troubles we have with the changes in our culture. Rather, our cultural concerns are most fixedly written on the cultural wall in best-selling non-fiction and fiction books and in film. One thinks immediately of classics like Upton Sinclair's *The Jungle* as well as more recent best-selling books such as *Reviving Ophelia: Saving the Selves of Adolescent Girls* by Mary Pipher and Ruth Ross, and (a personal favorite) Elizabeth Wurtzle's *Bitch: In Praise of Difficult Women.* There are, of course, hundreds of academic books and works of popular fiction and non-fiction about virtual culture and the concerns surrounding it. Several of the better of the lot, such as Scott Bukatman's *Terminal Identity* and James Gee's highly influential *What Videogames Have to Teach us About Learning and Literacy* (2003). But, all of these works are consumed by specific audiences and the impact on the broader culture is often limited and slow. Not everyone reads philosophy or cultural theory, or even fiction regularly. Of those who do read fiction, for example, the chances that they will read a science fiction novel such as William Gibson's *Neuromancer* is very, very small.

Film and television (what I will collectively refer to as "video"), however, have a very broad popular appeal and attempt, in the "Hollywood" incarnations, to be all-inclusive. Certainly it would be strange to find anyone in the United States today who has not at least heard of Michael Creighton, for example, but it is more likely this is due to having seen his name on television advertising a new movie or television show. What were "film" and "television" respectively are now multi-media projects as one work may run in the theaters, on television, be made available on VHS, DVD, and Blue-Ray, and even more recently, right on the computer screen or hand-held device via the internet. Contemporary video is part and parcel with the virtual revolution and it is, therefore, not surprising that one of the concerns of contemporary video productions, and particularly in cinema, is the increasingly virtual nature of our culture.

Cinema has always been a self-reflexive media. Like the history of drama demonstrates a tendency to reveal itself as artifice and to explore the means of creation, so cinema has always expressed concern with the methods of its own making. If in drama "life is a dream" and "the world's a stage," in cinema life becomes a flickering construction of light that can eternalize a moment, save it as if seen by human eyes, to be repeated again and again. In a sense, films are time-machines that fling captured moments forward through time for future viewing. From the start, the impulse of cinema was the creation of a virtual experience, a recorded sort of life that could fully envelop the participant. Despite the limitation of early cinema, the common folk evidenced a compelling interest in, what film scholar Robert Sklar, author of *Movie Made America*, describes as, the "pleasure and vicarious power" of the "mastery over time and motion" represented by early black and white cinema and Thomas Edison himself dreamed of a future "total cinema" that would completely surround and immerse the viewer participant.[23]

98

From its very conception cinema was in the business of making time and place asynchronous. No live actors danced about the stage, but analog representations composed of photographs and light recorded at one place and time and then replayed at a later place and time certainly supported the idea that bodies could become eternal in a sense just like traditional narrative and drama propelled personas into the future. In narrative and drama the essence of a person—their mythical, archetypal quality—could survive the physical death of the body. Telling and hearing the story, playing the character, or seeing the performance invoked the soul of individuals long dead. Even more, narrative—whether printed, verbal, or enacted—could serve as a creative force, manifesting personas that had never actually been. The main function of cinema was three-fold: to transmit actual events across space and time for future viewers (like the boxing matches of Jack Johnson for example), to likewise transport traditional narratives in visual format to a broader audience more cheaply than traditional theater could, and to create new narratives specifically designed for the new media.

Some of cinema's earliest subjects embraced this third option utilizing the uniquely asynchronous elements of cinema to produce visual wonders impossible to present in any other media. Due to this ability to portray events that had never been and scenes that could only be imagined it should not be surprising that science fiction, and I use the term loosely here to cover the fantastic and various forms of futurism, would quickly become one of the major subjects of early film. *Voyage danse la Lune* (1902), *The Cabinet of Doctor Caligheri* (1920), *Metropolis* (1927), all classics of early cinema, explored and worried over the impact of strange, new technologies on our culture, including the impact of cinema itself to potentially alter that reality. That the science fiction film continued after the early years primarily in the "B" pulp films is more a testament to its enduring popularity with audiences, and particularly young males, than a sign that it was not valued at all. The cost of special effects

---

[23] Sklar 17.

has always been a factor in the making of films and never more so than in SF films where an entire future or past often needs to be built from the ground up. In the case of the "B" movies, of course, even a card table and a curtain backdrop could become a spaceship as in *Plan 9 from Outer Space* (1956), which just goes to prove that SF themes were popular enough that a film featuring a guy in gorilla suit wearing a deep-sea diving helmet could turn a profit and continue, even to this day, to be seen by audiences, though obviously for different reasons than on initial release.

In general, science fiction narratives broke down the previous dependence of narrative upon the past, as in mythology, and the immediate future, as in logistical planning. What the people of Ur or ancient Athens would have seen as prognostication became, in SF, a form of logical projection, supposedly based in the methods of natural philosophy. We can see in Socrates' discussion of the perfect republic, which Plato wrote down around 500 BC, the origins of the film the *World of Tomorrow*, but the emphasis has shifted from what human nature is capable of to how our tools and methods, our technologies and sciences, are capable of doing for us in the case of utopian visions, or to us when imagining dystopias. How many of us have in some way been disappointed that we do not all have personal flying machines or that, while waiting in an airport, that teleporters have not yet been invented? These desires, however whimsical, demonstrate the incorporation of futurism, and SF, into the popular psyche. A homeless man I met in the subway once told me he wished "the government would go ahead and put those damned food replicators where everyone could get at them." Replicated food was OK by him. Most of us would love to have a food replicator, and that desire hides the fear of the reality that millions of people all over the world are starving to death—even in our own streets here in the USA.

In the sci-fi film, our fears and desires born of an increasingly technology dependent existence play out for the masses to see; and increasingly, these films directly explore our concern with the virtual nature of our lived reality. Long before millions of players spent countless hours playing *World of Warcraft* together in simulated spaces, SF film commodified the cultural concern that cyberspace was coming to get us, if it had not already done so and we somehow failed to notice except in our dreams and nightmares.

The art of cinema has always been concerned with its own artifice—with the means of production that result in an artificial or simulated reality. We can see this "self-reflexivity" even in early films where films were made about filmmaking or included shots with a camera at work. Like its most obvious predecessors—drama, painting, and photography—filmmakers are understandably engaged with the means of production of their art form. I've already mention Calderon de la Barca's play *Life is a Dream*, but there are many more examples of self-reflexive drama. For example, In his bestselling *Shakespeare: The Invention of the Human*, the inimitable Harold Bloom tags Shakespeare's *Hamlet* as the moment in history when we first see "modern man" emerge (in my phrasing) in his full self-reflexive neurotic glory. Certainly the play is rife with allusions to the artificial nature of human endeavor most famously demonstrated in the "play within a play" where Hamlet writes a play called "The Mousetrap" based on what his father's ghost has told him about Claudius' treacherous murder. When "The Mousetrap" is performed within the play *Hamlet* a stage is set upon the stage, real-life actors performing actors in *Hamlet* perform other characters in "The Mousetrap," and the actors playing the court of Elsinore become an audience on the stage upon which they perform and the audience in the theater becomes an audience watching the performance of an audience who is watching a play be performed for them. The immediate effect of the play within a play is immersive: to make the audience forget briefly, as they watch parts of "The Mousetrap" before Hamlet interrupts, that they are already watching a play called *Hamlet*. The actors who play actors in *Hamlet* inevitably perform "The Mousetrap" in a staged, awkward, "older" style so that the performers of the court of Elsinore seem more "real" by comparison. Yet, this device of immersion also calls into question the "reality" of the audience. If the audience on the stage watching "The Mousetrap" is not really an audience—if they are merely (and nightly) performing their roles as Hamlet and

Claudius and Gertrude and Ophelia then who (or what) are the members of the audience? Do they "perform" their roles as well? When actors play actors in a play who perform characters in a play within a play and, even more convoluted, when a boy actor can play girl character who cross-dress as a boy and then pretends to be, or "acts like" a girl for another male actor-character (as in Shakespeare's *Twelfth Night*), the where, exactly does the "core" of the persona--indeed, the very nature of reality—lie? When, as Puck asserts in Shakespeare's *Midsummer's Night Dream*, that "All the world's a stage," he is actually suggesting that all of human culture is a performance of roles, a never ending simulation, and that what theater *does* is draw attention to that fact by being more overtly constructed. The pleasure we draw from theater, then, is not simply the pleasure of the voyeur who looks into rooms as a silent and hidden observer, but also the pleasure of watching reality being *intentionally* constructed word by word and movement by movement just as we suspect our lives are likewise constructed through innumerable performances let loose into the world—though regrettably sans a writer or director. Drama, in this sense, mirrors life, but reconstitutes it in a more logical fashion where all makes some kind of sense. Like a game, drama pleasantly confines reality while at the same time showing reality itself to be a type of game that has, by comparison, spun wildly out of control. This self-reflexivity, or feed-back loop, that questions the very nature of "human reality," or "culture," as a consensual hallucination is what continues to make drama—be it on stage, screen, television, in the park, or parking lot—a popular medium of performance. We enjoy watching the intentional simulation play out, dropped lines and all, because we see in the *intentional* practiced performance a mirror of our lived existence and we take those performances with us back out into the world as exemplars for our lives, as was the intention of the first formal dramatic performances which were on religious themes.

There are numerous examples of this tendency toward self-reflexivity in the plastic arts as well. In his book *The Order of*

Things: An Archaeology of the Human Sciences,[24] French philosopher Michel Foucault, for example, points to Diego Velázquez's painting *Las Meninas* (Spanish for "The maids of honor").

Painted in 1656, *Las Meninas* is a study in simulation and audience. In the frame of the painting we see a room and, filling the room, from left to right, we see the back of an enormous canvas; a painter,

[24] Michel Foucault, *The Order of Things: An Archaeology of the Human Sciences*, (New York: Random House, 1970).

Velázquez himself in fact, looking out of the picture apparently at us. In his poised hands are brush and palette and he seems just in the act of preparing to make a stroke on the canvas. Beside Velázquez are five figures: historically we know these are the five year old Infanta (Spanish for "princess") Margarita and her maids of honor, doña Isabel de Velasco and doña María Agustina Sarmiento de Sotomayor. To the right of the princess are two court dwarves, a stout female, Maribarbola, and a tiny male, the court clown Nicolas Pertusato, whose foot rests playfully on an apparently dosing mastiff. A bit behind the five figures stand the Infanta's chaperone, doña Marcela de Ulloa talking to an unidentified bodyguard; and on the back wall a man, the Queen's Chamberlain, Don José Nieto Velázquez, is in the act of looking back at the scene as he is exiting the room up a flight of stairs. And, most strangely, in a mirror on the back wall we see reflected the upper body of two small figures: King Philip IV of Spain and Queen Mariana de Austria, who are the supposed "subjects" of the painting Velázquez is working on in the painting.[25] I have seen this painting in the Prado museum in Madrid, and it is a most impressive and disturbing sight. The overall effect is that almost everyone in the painting is looking at *you* and that Velázquez is painting *you*. Then, when I saw the mirror in the back, as anyone who stands there for a few moments must as it is just left and below the exact center of the work, I had this strange sense that one of those people was me and that my partner and I looked like that; and for more than instant, I was transported back in time and space to Velázquez's studio in Philip IV's Alcázar palace in Madrid. The effect was quite disturbing and I shall never forget it as long as I live. In fact, I still feel a strange disorientation when I look at the tiniest reproduction of the painting.

The temporal and spatial disturbance that views of *Las Meninas* often feel is due to the fact that Velázquez's work is not simply a painting of a subject but a painting whose subject is the act of

---

[25] There is some disagreement among art critics as to whether the mirror reflects the actual King and Queen or the painting on the canvas that Velázquez is working on.

creating, of making art itself. Like a "snapshot," Velázquez has captured a "moment" in time—but *Las Meninas* is more than this: Velázquez has not only captured a moment, he has created or constructed a moment and created an impossible viewpoint all at once. Unlike an almost instantaneous Polaroid or digital photo, it would have taken months for Velázquez to complete *Las Meninas* and, therefore, the scene we see in the painting is a "moment" assembled from numerous sittings of the different participants at different times and perhaps even in other locales. The artist, Velázquez, has placed himself into the frame and, therefore, also leaves the "position" or the artists' gaze "empty" for viewer to fill. When looking at the painting we are in the position of both the subject of the unnamed work on the canvas in the frame, the subject the painted Velázquez's "gaze," and the figures indicated in the mirror. We are also in the position that would have been occupied by Velázquez himself as he painted *Las Meninas*—the traditional position of the viewer and artist. As Foucault suggests, the back of the canvas indicates this confused identity, and "we do not know who we are, or what we are doing."[26]

Drama and painting are technologies of simulation and techniques of reality production which, at the same time as they simulate and produce realities, comment more or less directly on the artifice of our lived experience. Similarly, photography simulates reality by making a "copy" of what may be seen with the eye and inscribing or transferring the visual information onto one or more media such as the film, hard-drive, paper, and computer screen for later viewing. But at the same time, photography assists in the production of reality and even produces a reality all its own. Unlike painting with its assemblage of "moments," the photograph really is what we call a "snapshot"—a single captured moment in time. It might be posed, the image can certainly be fiddled with and altered in a myriad of ways, but the very idea of the photograph is that moment that Velázquez aimed for in *Las Meninas*. We can see the

---

[26] Foucault, *The Order of Things*, 5.

dual function of the photograph when we think about human memory.

When I see a photo of my college days, for example, of me at 23 (much thinner, of course) and my friends camping at Turner Falls in Oklahoma, the photo not only serves as a reminder of a moment, but actually helps re-create the moment itself. Even more, the exact moment in the photo may have long been lost in the myriad of moments at Turner Falls and over the course of the many I have lived years since and yet the photo becomes that lost moment and replaces it. When I think of Turner Falls now, one of the things I "remember" is the photo itself and I would never think to doubt its veracity like I would my own recollection! In many ways the photograph is the reality just as much as my own memories which are often confused and subject to negotiation with my friends; "No, you were back at camp." "That happened on another camping trip." "That was the time Nisa whacked you hard with one of those play swords we made out of broomsticks."

Finally, I would like to point out that like *Las Meninas*, photos are also narratives in the sense that they invite the production of narratives. When I see a picture of myself at Turner Falls I immediately begin to construct narratives about it, in both the sense of "on the subject" and "around the subject," or, if you prefer, *through it*. It makes sense then, that once the technology began to improve the speed at which photos could be taken, that photographers, lining up a series of photos taken over a short period time, would be drawn to the fragmented movement of the captured bodies through the captured spaces and begin to desire to simulate more than just the moment. The narrative, as it were, the *story*, was already there in the image, waiting to be freed, like the Venus of Willendorf from her rock.

There are many excellent histories of cinema and I will, therefore, simply point out here the very basic fact that what we call "movies" are, as the name implies, a series of photographic images that, shown in rapid succession, produce the illusion of movement across a two dimensional surface. Actual space and time are simulated for the eye, but, like the simple photograph itself invites the narrative, movies also produce spaces and times. We enjoy the artifice of the simulation but at the same time the reality-producing mechanisms of the machine stir deep fears in our collective unconscious. Wonder and fear walk hand and hand across the flickering reality of the silver screen and the screen itself becomes, like the rock walls of Lascaux, the veil between ourselves and that other immortal world where bodies do not age and die only once but live again and again in their immortal forms. Actors like Marilyn Monroe are not immortal in merely name, but immortal in simulated space. I can see Marilyn talk and walk and breathe and sing in the movie theater, on TV, on my computer screen. She, like the famous actors of the theater, is not merely *immortalized* in memory (though she is certainly that) she is immortalized in the simulation, canonized by the artifice, a reality born unto itself, "Marilyn Monroe," that unforgettable omnipresent avatar of the sweet girl Norma Jean Baker, who died and left her ever-running performances behind to continue on without her.

The films which serve up the very essence of the fascination with the boundary between the theater or the living room and the world on the other side of the screen I have decided to call "virtual cinema" because the core of these films is the anxiety about the permeability of the screen itself and the reality of the world on the other side. What follows is not a history of virtual cinema, though I have chosen a chronological pattern, and I do not have the space here for a discussion of every film that might fall under the heading of "virtual cinema," so I will discuss the ones that seem most relevant to the discussions in the final chapters of this book and attempt to mention as many other relevant titles as I can along the way.

Certainly, as I mentioned previously, there are numerous films about the making films. Much less common, until very recently, are films concerned with the juxtaposition of public spaces and private spaces with cinema space, or more broadly termed, virtual space. By public and private spaces I mean simply the spaces we occupy when we physically are alone or physically with other people or when we feel ourselves to be alone or with others. These spaces are both literal, as in my living room, and psychological as in when I am writing and enter "the zone" (or what my partner calls "the cave" when I fail to respond to questions such as "Why is the house on fire?"). Virtual space, as I intend the term here, plays out on surfaces that are being used as "screens"—in the movie theater, on television, on my computer, PowerPoint projections on the wall in my classrooms, on the small screens of cell phones, and iPods. Even my body has been used as a screen, or as part of a screen, on numerous occasions. As I move about New York City, particularly in malls, museums, the larger subway stations, and tourist centers, projections play across my body as I walk through them and for a moment I become the screen, a piece of the wall between this world and the one on the other side.

This anxiety about the reality of the projection on the screen plays out in small ways in many films—most of us have seen a movie where a scene is acted out in a dark movie theater such as in *The Player* (1992), *Far from Heaven*(2002), and *Annie Hall*(1977). Often, someone stands on the stage in front of the projection, or we see their shadow from behind the screen as they run past, or even get shot behind or through the screen. More obvious, but less frequent, are the films where the characters actually enter or leave the movie screen. We might think of *The Purple Rose of Cairo* (1985), *Last Action Hero* (1993), or, for the "B" movie crowd, *Dead End Drive In* (1986), or the "be considerate to others" advertisement that preceded films in certain theaters that had Inspector Clouseau (in this case, the animated version) sneaking into the theater and apparently tearing through the movie screen. There are ample examples of interaction with television screens as well such as *Poltergeist* (1982) where the little girl, Carol Anne Freeling, is apparently sucked into the TV and, more recently, an episode of *Charmed* titled "Chick Flick" (April 20, 2000) where two onscreen killers emerge from the TV to wreak havoc and humor at the expense of the movie industry.

These moments where the screen, and its illusions, are troubled by intruding bodies presage the advent of virtual cinema where the virtual space itself—the illusory space projected on the screen—becomes a realm that may be entered through the flickering-light, magical door that leads to Oz, Wonderland, the Moon, Mars, or Cleveland, and any of the other fantastical, impossible spaces created by the camera. I say "impossible spaces" because the camera stands in like the point of view of *Las Meninas* and "sees" for us while taking up impossible positions within those magical spaces. The camera even enters the virtual bodies themselves—we sometimes "see" through one or another character's eyes so that we, the audience, apparently "stand in" for the missing body of the actor.[27] We, the audience, can "see" from anywhere, though in film and television we do not control where the "anywhere" will be. This lack of control over the point of view and our inability to directly participate in the narrative is why we generally call film and television "passive media".

As previously discussed, however, video games did allow us to make things happen on the screen, and shortly after the videogame revolution began, films began to reflect or concern over this newly invented power to make things happen in what William Gibson famously termed as "cyberspace". Released in 1982, *Tron* had its origins in the videogame *Pong*. As *Tron*'s writer-director Steven Lisberger claims, after seeing a film of the action in *Pong*, "I realized that there were these techniques that would be very suitable for bringing video games and computer visuals to the screen. And that was the moment that the whole concept flashed across my mind".[28] In *Tron*, in case you missed seeing it, computer programmer Kevin Flynn's body is "digitized" into the computer by an experimental transporter/food replicator-like device which is designed to store and transmit objects through computer connections (i.e. the internet). In the digital realm, Flynn encounters a physical manifestation of programs in virtual three-dimensional

---

[27] Film theorists refer to this change of perspective into and out of the point of view of one of the characters as a "suture". See, for example, Annette Kuhn's summary of the subject in *Women's Pictures* (New York: Verso, 1982) 53-56.

[28] Patterson, Richard Patterson, "The Making of *Tron*" (*American Cinematographer*, August 1982).

spaces. The digital spaces ostensibly represent the actual hardware of the computer itself.

The "evil computer tries to take over the world" premise for *Tron* was certainly nothing new, the most critically noticed prior example being *Colossus: The Forbin Project* (1970). As with *Colossus,* in *Tron* we see exposed the fear that computers or computer programs may become sentient, that they may somehow drag us into their world, and that they would not only enslave us, but force us to wear really stupid glowing neon outfits. Regardless of questionable costuming choices, the metaphor acted out in *Tron* is one of the player's strong engagement with a computer game. Engagement in this case leads to a literal disembodiment and re-embodiment as a digitized avatar. The player is erased and the avatar and game become the reality. Thus, though *Tron* is essentially an anthropomorphic video game-player's fantasy, it does belie several conditions of video game play.

- Players may feel disembodied while playing a game.
- The two dimensional screen may be perceived as real space.
- Players may feel re-embodiment within the game space which is perceived as real three-dimensional.
- Avatars and other characters within the game, and the programs they graphically represent, may be perceived as being "alive" and as exhibiting choice and free will.

That the *Tron* video game was released at virtually the same time as the film heightens the sense of virtual embodiment. The desire to be in the cinematic space created on the screen transfers to the game play experience where the player executes control over the avatar that represents the protagonist of the film. Even more, as the game follows the narrative structure of the film, the sense of disembodiment and virtual space actually posits the game player *as the protagonist* of the film so that the player experiences the game as an interactive version of the film where playing is reviewing the film from the inside. Or, to restate, since the film posits the protagonist as literally being pulled into the computer (itself a metaphor for game play) this reinforces the sense that the player is also being "pulled into" the computer, or disembodied, during game play.

Thus *Tron*, as a cinematic artifact, marks the moment where the boundaries between real and virtual, cinema and game, observer and observed, and viewer and protagonist are simultaneously assaulted. William Gibson's *Neuromancer* published a few years later (1984) may get the credit for the naming of cyberspace but *Tron*—in its simultaneous manifestation as both game and film—was the first real popularizer of the collapsing boundary between VR and RL. Not only could we see it, we could be it. What's more, we liked it. It would, however, be just over ten more years before the virtual really came alive on the big screen.

1995 was supposed to be a banner year for cyberpunk and virtuality in Hollywood. *Virtuosity* (1995), *Strange Days* (1995), and William Gibson's own *Johnny Mnemonic* (1995) all hit the theaters to quite a lot of hoopla but little audience return. However, each introduced a new theme for the virtual subject into the theaters: namely the escape of the evil AI from the computer, the obsession with virtualized experience, and the human become cyborg.

The virtually irredeemable film *Virtuosity* plays on the *Tron* trope of virtual games combined with the now popular conception of Gibson's cyberspace but quickly inverts the source of fear from the entering of cyberspace itself to AI escaping into the real world. Again utilizing a *Star Trek* favorite, though this time from TNG, Sid 6.0 escapes from cyberspace and into a body constructed entirely of nanites (microscopic computer robots). However, the much more interesting scenes in an otherwise typical and sub-par action flick, despite the best efforts of Denzel Washington and a young Russell Crowe, are before Sid escapes. The opening scenes are of a virtually constructed urban area that is somewhat glitchy.

When Sid kills his virtual partner and almost kills him as well, Barnes ultimately feels free to "kill" a virtual innocent bystander in order to shut down Sid because "its only a game." This act, we soon learn, is a mirror of the supposed crime Barnes committed in the real world that landed him in prison. Once Sid gets out into the real world, however, Barnes begins to see Sid's homicidal actions as still being part of the game which expresses the fear that computer games and cyberspace can somehow "leak out" into our world and directly affect change whether that change be for good or ill. Though obviously based to some extent on AI films, and in particular on lethal simulation films like War Games where simulations threaten to become real and destroy the world, *Virtuosity* explores not simply the loss of control over our own machines (essentially a Cold-War fear of thermonuclear war) but rather the eroding boundary between man and the smart machine.

To highlight this eroding boundary between the flesh and technology, we learn that Barnes has a robotic arm-an ancestor technology and analogue to Sid's own nanite body. Man has already been infiltrated by the machine, man is already entering cyberspace and feeling the physical effects of it, now the AI escapes out into the world and brings at least a little of cyberspace with it. Perhaps the most interesting thing about this otherwise horrid film is the use of shots which intersect the virtual and the real. These Max Headroom-esque images belie a similar fear to *Tron*: that somehow those people we see on TV really live in there and we might be sucked into the screen as well.

Referencing *Star Trek: The Next Generation*'s popular and disturbing "Ship in a Bottle" episode (#138 January 24 1993) where the virtual criminal Moriarty is unwittingly trapped in a program that simulates the real world, Sid is ultimately defeated in his homicidal obsession with Barnes by destroying his nanite body and then tricking him into thinking cyberspace is real. *Virtuosity* ends with an image of Sid trapped in a cyberspace hell before Barnes casts his memory chip out over the city. *Star Trek*'s own relationship with virtual environments is as enduring as it is convoluted. The joys and pitfalls of AI was a popular theme in the original series of *Star Trek* beginning with the Enterprise's own computer. In TNG, however, the holodeck becomes a major setting and is featured as a primary plot device in numerous episodes. In the very first episode we meet both the amazing android Data and the wondrous holodeck in the same scene. We should not forget, they both really were amazing and wondrous; and their juxtaposition even more so. For the first time, the mechanical robot occupies the virtual landscape.

In *Strange Days* (1995), recorded events take the place of real life and the protagonist, an ex-cop named Lenny, is caught in his own past, addicted to the virtual recordings of a love affair that has long since ended. Thanks to technology, memories become experiences that can be replayed over and over again and, therefore, do not fade over time. Lenny believes that the virtual experience— based on his apparent addiction to recordings of himself with his ex-girlfriend—is the real world and the Faith who dumped him for a rich rock star the "fake" Faith. His obsessive replaying, or reliving, of his recorded experiences with her is what leads him down the wrong path. You cannot, the film is clearly saying, hold on to the past and to do so is to lose your sense of the now. For all the technological hoo-ha in the film, the basis seems to be little more than an extension of a similar scene in *Bladerunner* (1982).

However, whereas Deckerd chooses a synthetic woman over his memory, Lenny will eventually choose a real woman (Angela Basset's "Mace" Mason) over the virtual one, a recurrent theme in science fiction from *Spacehunter: Adventures in the Forbidden Zone* (1983) to *Cherry 2000* (1987). The film seems to say that not only has Lenny lost himself in a fake past (the memories not fading as they ought) but that the machine itself has somehow stolen Faith's soul. In this scene she is nude and natural, while in a later scene on stage in the "now" she is scantily clad but clearly artificial and *lewd*. This technology, the film seems to imply, has stolen something from them and reduced both to something no longer quite human and clearly inferior. Also noteworthy is Angela Basset's role as "Mace" Mason, as the first cyberpunk female action adventure hero of color. The casting belies an early interest in race in the cyberpunk film: an interest no doubt picked up from Gibson's own race concerns in his stories.

And then there was *Johnny Mnemonic* (1995) starring Keanu Reeves. The tension in *Johnny Mnemonic* derives from Johnny's implanted memory that he uses to house secret information for a price. His cyborg self proves less than beneficial, however, when his memory is overloaded and he faces death if he cannot download the information quickly enough. The central theme in *Johnny* is the infiltration of the flesh by technology.

Technological infiltration and minorities seem to go hand in hand in *Johnny* though the references are ideologically complex. For example, *Johnny*, like *Strange Days*, included a tough female, Jane (Dina Meyer), who is clearly based in William Gibson's own Molly Millions female assassin archetype who uses technology to enhance herself in order to compete more closely with men or even exceed them physically. But in this case, this competition comes at both a high physical and social price.

And who can forget Ice-T, who in the same year played a genetically altered kangaroo resistance fighter in *Tank Girl* (1995) as the minority resistance fighter in *Johnny*? Though in *Tank Girl* Ice-T plays a mutant Kangaroo, the idea here is basically the same: minorities (and quite often African-Americans) are the ones who save us from ourselves in the technological future. In *Johnny*, his companion is a technologically enhanced dolphin created by the military to seek out submarines. Finally, it is easy for many of us to forget that Keanu Reeves was himself considered quite the minority actor when *Johnny Mnemonic* hit the screens, but many early reviewers commented on his then "obvious" mixed heritage.

Though this visual association of technology and the bodies of political minorities could be read in many different ways, by my reading these images represent the literalization—a literal embodiment—of technologies of control while at the same time suggesting that wrenching the technology away from the power structures can serve as a means of empowerment. This is the same notion that Donna J. Haraway will elucidate in her seminal, and oft quoted, article "A Cyborg Manifesto."[29]

Though not living in a computer realm, *The Truman Show* (1998) posits one man's life as a virtual construction. Mostly

---

[29] Donna J. Haraway, *Simians, Cyborgs and Women: The Reinvention of Nature.* New York: Routledge, 1991.

114

voyeuristic in intent, *The Truman Show* gives us the story of a man raised in a Disney-World like small town where everyone smiles and everyone loves him. What he does  not know is that his world is a lie and the "real world" is watching. (Note how once again the importance of the face on, or in, the television screen which belies our desire to be inside that virtual world). When we see Truman standing in front of the bathroom mirror imagining himself leading a more interesting life a la *It's a Wonderful Life* or *The Secret Lives of Walter Mitty*, his personal entertainments becomes our entertainment. But we also see him *through* the glass: a camera perspective that puts us in the position of seeing ourselves as Truman. Thus as we watch Truman in his daily life we become increasingly aware that the real implication of the film is that we all may live a life analogous to Truman's. Truman's reality serves as a metaphor for our own feeling that reality, as such, is not really real but manufactured. Or, in good Marxist terms, that we are all the products of a technologically supported ideology. What are we afraid of as expressed in *The Truman Show*? We cannot know the real world. Our life is not what we think or wish. We are always being watched. Everyone lies to us.

But at least Truman had the satisfaction that escape was seemingly possible. And at the end of the film, he enjoys a moment of satisfaction at reaching the end of his world before entering the next. And we might note the Christian death symbolism of stairway to heaven here.

With the release of *The Matrix* in 1999, being virtual became cool. The premise for *The Matrix* (directed by Andy and Larry Wachowski) could easily be read as a sequel to the AI takes over the world film *Colossus: the Forbin Project* (1970): sometime around the beginning of the 21st century, men invented Artificial

Intelligence. Something went wrong and the machines rebelled against their creators. Human beings then did something cataclysmic to the environment in order to create a permanent cloud-cover blocking out the sunlight and, thereby, the machine's primary source of energy. The machines then captured all of humanity and turned them into biological batteries. In order to keep the humans from staging their own rebellion (or dying in their tubes) the machines created a virtual space known as The Matrix (from Gibson's coinage) which replicates the late 20th century for the imprisoned humans. When the film opens, whole generations of human beings have been born and died in captivity all the while believing themselves to be living in the glass and glitter of an unnamed Urban Area (there is no mention of a virtual suburbia or of rural areas). Life, it seems, is indeed a dream. Earth has become Hell and the devil at the helm an AI program of our own devising.

The fear is amplified in *The Matrix Reloaded* (2003) and *The Matrix Revolutions* (2003) to more strongly assault the boundary between the human and the machine, between the real and the virtual, may not be quite as clear cut as it seems. The advertising poster itself implies the digital nature of the main characters and several key scenes serve to undermine the notion of a "real" at all. The Marxist proposition here is evident: capitalism is a device of control, a consensual illusion that keeps us from realizing, from seeing, how ugly the world is and that humans have become little more than slaves to intelligent machines (which we may read as a synecdoche for power and power structures in the Foucauldian sense). Ironically, the "real" future is not the one we would wish to have. It is a post-apocalyptic nightmare of bad clothing and glop for every meal. However, it is racially diverse as seen in this shot. At least in the cyberpunk film, minorities do survive into the future.

The future we fetishize is The Matrix: to know what The Matrix is and be able to dominate it. To bend the rules and even break them as Neo does. This is the real promise of cyberspace since Gibson— freedom from the confines of the body. But like any fetish, it also hides the source of the fear: that we have already been dominated and controlled and we somehow failed to notice.

The virtual projection of our mental selves matches pretty closely with the real world body. And I have to wonder, before his release how did Neo know what he looked like? Or even more to the point, considering the desiccated cyborg body that is the "real" Mr. Anderson, how does he know what he *should* look like? And why does he never imagine himself entirely as he is with his implants, bad sweaters, etc. Why not a woman? In this case, cyberspace apparently restricts self-expression in a way that we do not see on the Internet now.

What we do see in The Matrix is that we may become faster, stronger, certainly better dressed, in cyberspace. And, apparently this is what we all wish for.

Race, sex, gender, and body style are all apparently essential, though of these we see an increased tendency to erase race in humans. All humans have become somewhat "ethnic" and by the same token, all their avatars in The Matrix have become somewhat more white. As you can see in these four posters, the major indicator of ethnicity would appear to be colored clothing and the guns. The only real white guy is Smith. The agents of the machines are the evil whites embodied in the image of Agent Smith. Who spreads like a disease and threatens to take over the world of The Matrix and even threatens to escape it. Whiteness is contagious and lethal. But even Smith and Neo are constantly compared to one another both in image, action and word. Ultimately, *The Matrix* implies that indeed, as Calderon de la Barca pointed out almost 400 years ago "Life is indeed a Dream" no matter what level of implementation you are operating on.

The strongest impulse of the latter two installments is the slippage in the distinction between the real world and The Matrix. Neo, however, is able to somehow infiltrate her virtual body with his own and save her life both in The Matrix and out. His actions in The Matrix alter what happens in the real world. He somehow manages to correct her data self thus saving her supposedly meat self. Neo also has similar powers in the real world. One possibility is that Neo is able to communicate with The Matrix from the real world without a connection. As all the machines are tied to The

117

Matrix, he can contact them through it even subconsciously. However, the film does not seem to support this reading as we "see" waves of power emanating from him in the real world. Thus, the only reading directly supported by the evidence in the film is that the real world is also a matrix, or *The Matrix*, though at a higher level of implementation. As the saying goes, its "Turtles all the way down." Here we see Neo seeing the supposedly real world even though he was recently blinded. His new vision makes the Real World look very much like his "special vision" within The Matrix.

In *S1m0ne* (2002), by contrast, the virtual world begins to take over the real one starting with one mysterious, beautiful, and talented actress who is the invention of two men. The protagonist of *S1m0ne*, director Viktor Transki (played by Al Pacino), is fed up with the shenanigans of real life actresses and falls into despair. Then he is accosted by an apparent crazy man (Hank, played by Elias Koteas) who turns out to have created the perfect virtual reality actress creation program, and Viktor ends up with the power to make the perfect star. Desperate for a hit, he creates S1m0ne (or "Simone") and she is an instantaneous world-wide hit and even "launches" a successful singing career with "live" performances. Again we see the importance of the imagery of the face in the Screen to define both the fetish of the created being and the fear that we ourselves are created or outmoded by the creation. The TV screen simultaneously lends both credibility to the image and indicates control of the image.

Ultimately, however, the fetish must be destroyed or it takes over the world. Unlike Sid in *Virtuosity*, however, Simone turns out to be quite the survivor. After staging her supposed retirement in seclusion, Viktor uses a computer virus to delete her program only to find out that he is suspected of her murder. When he confesses to his role in creating Simone, the world simply will not believe that their experience of Simone was not real. He must then resurrect Simone with the help of his ex-wife and daughter. Finally, the virtual world integrates even more fully into the real world as Viktor and Simone form a VR/RL nuclear family with virtual babies and all.

Even more bizarre is the Jim Carey/Kate Winslet vehicle, *Eternal Sunshine of the Spotless Mind* (2004) which serves as a comic counterpoint to *Strange Days*. Like *Strange Days* the computer enters the mind rather than the mind entering the computer. But in this case the mind is treated exactly like any other computer. Memories, like programs, can be merely erased.

The story is simple, really. Boy and girl fall in love. Boy and girl break up. Boy finds out that said girl has had all memories of him permanently erased from her mind and he decides to undergo the same process. What he does not know is that he will re-live his memories of his life with her from the last to the first meeting as the procedure is carried out. As the memories of Clementine begin to peel away one by one, Joel decides that he cannot bear the thought of living without even the memory of her. He begins, at her suggestion, to hide her in other memories with some disturbing (albeit comical) effects. His mission becomes clear: he must save Clementine—or at least her memory—from destruction. (In Jungian terms, we might say that he is saving what amounts to his own Anima from the destructive impulse of technology.) Memories intermingle and merge as the Doctor's team seeks out the "renegade" memories of Clementine. Ultimately, however, they cannot escape and she is finally erased completely, though that is not quite the end of the story.

Films focusing on virtual reality seem to share is a preoccupation with the potential for the virtual to infiltrate and replace our "real" lives. *The Matrix*, following *The Truman Show*, even goes so far as to suggest that our real lives may not be real at all, or that the virtual may be just as real as anything else. Ultimately, the view of these technologies expressed in the Hollywood film is the same: they pervert us, enslave us, and make us something less than we ought to be, less than human. In these films, the virtual world of the computer steals our very soul. However, what we see may be a bit more complex: we have a deeply rooted fear of the virtual that is historically rooted in the fear of woman. This fear of the castrating power of technology is displaced into fetish. Thus, technology is both our destroyer and our savior, our enemy and our lover. It turns us into machines, takes away all emotion (especially love) and yet, ironically, allows love to bloom like a flower on a dungheap.

Nine: iPorn

"The internet is for Porn!" –*Avenue Q*

Internet pornography is, in most respects, little different from the more mundane variety that has been known, and often admired, throughout history. The main differences being ease of access, the wide variety of styles and tastes that are catered to, and in some cases, interaction. The ease of access to internet pornography, and its proliferation, has been the cause of concern almost since the day the internet went up, but pornography itself is ancient and the enjoyment of sexual materials can be traced to back to our Venus of Willendorf that could easily have been masturbatory materials for a sexual rite. Internet pornography is certainly easily accessible and a cause of concern especially in regards to children brought t up in a puritanical culture. We should not forget issues of power and degradation.

But my purpose here is not to critique the social benefits or ills of internet pornography or pornography in general. There is simply too much disagreement about it—including what constitutes pornography in the first place and what is simply erotic or art featuring nudes or what have you—for a lengthy discussion to be fruitful here. I am generally of the belief that the nude body and sex are entirely natural and, therefore, what constitutes the vast majority of materials considered pornography are not in themselves harmful to men or women. Pornography is the visual representation of male desire. The images come from the male psyche and will always be there as long as we live within a society based upon a two-sex model as defined by men. This is about patriarchal desire. Eliminating pornography does not eliminate the desire nor the forms that desire takes. Rather, pornography is an effect and not a cause of the two-sex model. This is to say again that abuses of power are always harmful and the pornography industry has long been the prevue of men. That is changing somewhat in the post-feminist era where former porn stars acquire doctorates and travel the globe with a vaginal speculum in hand to display their vaginas to the public as does Dr. Sally Sprinkle, and more and more so-called "amateur" models are making a decent living off of their own pay websites. Men certainly still predominate in the power structure, but the women are clearly gaining ground (Not to mention that the adult film industry is still the only venue where women have consistently higher salaries than men). Violence, however, is another matter altogether and violent behaviors, even when consensual, are not sex but something else altogether.

Which brings us to the second issue: the wide variety of sexual tastes depicted on the web. Again, one versant in pornography and sexual psychology is unlikely to find much new on the web that was not available through other media so again the real issue is availability. Certainly most of us had never seen images like those that may pop up on a simple web search with the word "sex." And many of these sites are extremely aggressive with a never-ending series of pop-up advertisements. The worst most of us would expect before the internet was an occasional *Playboy* advertisement or an *Adam and Eve* catalog in the mail. If you live in city like New York, New Orleans, Las Vegas, Paris, or London (or virtually any other large city in the world) then you would occasionally see prostitute cards littering the streets or escort advertisements in a local newspaper. Perhaps, depending on what part of town you were in, you would encounter a somewhat dubious establishment advertising "live sex acts onstage" with aging glossy photos yellowing in a scratched Plexiglas marquis or a disproportionate waspish figured drawing looming curiously on the front wall. In this respect the internet is quite different from our previous experience as a culture. Sex is there, it is everywhere, much of it is free, and the more exotic fetishes stand right alongside of the more tame soft-core varieties. One can quite easily run across such examples as the polymorphous Freudian nightmare of Tickle Me Elmo-heroin-foot-fetish insanity without much effort and, perhaps, with quite a bit of shame and disgust.

The internet is truly the subconscious of our culture. Whatever people think, whatever they really think, is there on the web somewhere no matter how fringe or counter-culture, or downright horrifying to the rest of us. I personally find white-supremacist and Neo-Nazi sites just as disturbing as the most vicious porn sites (which are sexist and generally racist as well). One is always tempted to laugh at a relatively harmless sexual fetish, but violence and hate are never funny and should never be taken as such.

Child pornography is also certainly unacceptable in a world culture where legal sexual maturity is based on an age and not psychological or sexual maturity. However, while some forms of child pornography, based on the "young nubile virgin" myth, are clearly admonished with a knowing patriarchal wink, other forms are considered with the worst of crimes and rightly so, for the "model" of child pornography (who cannot be considered "willing" in any social, psychological, sexual, or legal sense) is the subject of physical violence, psychological violence, and most often both. And again, violence is not sex but a blatant misuse of power and, therefore, reprehensible with the worst crimes of humanity.

Many would argue—as Naomi Wolff did in *New York Magazine*[30]—that the internet has created a nation of pornography addicts, but I would argue that if we want to discuss addiction (and I have never been happy with theories of addiction to begin with), I have been addicted during my life to many practices including writing, reading, playing online games (thus this book), and many other "harmless" activities. I literally get the shakes when I have not written for a few days, though I would read that, as Freud would, as guilt and not addiction. In any case, the argument that one becomes "addicted" to internet porn seems to me to be targeting a symptom and calling it the cause.

That Wolf's arguments center around her experience with college students should not be surprising for several reasons. 1) College is the first opportunity for most men to freely look at pornography. As adults, not only are they are able to legally buy pornography subscribe to adult websites, they also have the legal right to privacy in such matters. 2) That women *see* the men looking at pornography is simply a factor of the excessive freedom of the

---

[30] Naomi Wolff, *New York Magazine* (20 October 2003).

college undergraduate and actually indicative of another factor, access. Young women have access to the men's rooms and vice-versa. These days, many undergraduate couples live together and the male's pornography comes to the house with the old furniture. 3) That young college women are meeting young men who seem emotionally distant and yet obsessed with sex is not particularly shocking either and I doubt pornography has anything at all to do with many eighteen to twenty year old men behaving like jerks. What the women see in the pornographic image is not significantly different in effect from what they see everywhere else—even in women's magazines.

The guys who supposedly prefer internet pornography to the real thing are the same ones who have always done so—they are males with deeper intimacy issues of which pornography is a symptom, but not a cause. If pornography reduced male desire, we would also assume that the homosexual community would suffer the same effects. However, though gay men have the highest per capita consumption of pornography, they also have extremely active sexual lives. Admittedly, pornography may play a role in lowering male self-esteem particularly as regards their own body as the gay community is both notoriously body conscious and self-conscious. However, few would claim that pornography is the *cause* of either condition and is, rather, a visible symptom.

Perhaps Wolff's best case regards the personalization of iporn— if you can imagine it you can find it. If you can't find it, you can request it and, for a very small sum (usually less than $20) you can get it. You can even have live interactions with a live girl somewhere in the world who performs what you ask, but this is often little more than chat room and requires quite a lot of imagination and certainly more than I have.

The real cause of the problem is not pornography, on or off the internet, but the average young woman's self-esteem. They feel bad about their bodies and themselves. These feelings are completely understandable in a patriarchal culture, but they are not new, and eliminating pornography will not make them go away even if focusing on a culprit may relieve the pressure for a brief while. Neither will learning to be more coy.

The tone of alien-abduction, recovered memory—the incitement to panic is obvious: internet porn caused all my problems. Harkening back to an earlier era of masturbatory fears—hairy palms, impotency, eternal damnation—the current iporn frenzy is taking on the trappings of a witch hunt, and I hate to see such a well-known and respected feminist such as Naomi Wolff campaigning for restrictions on the 1st Amendment, restrictions on male and female sexuality, and restrictions on the possible permutations of sexual pleasure and sexual relationships. What Naomi Wolff seems to want is a return to good old-fashioned Reagan-Bush heterosexual monogamous relationships circa 1950 (or 1850) that never really existed in the first place.

iPorn is not our problem: AIDS, gay-bashing, sexual assault, date-rape and ruffies, child abuse (including child pornography), the homeless, bigotry, and the inability of a culture to recognize any form of long-term unions other than the heterosexual couple. Post-feminism—at least in the hands of one of the best-known of American feminists—does not sit well in this case. Women are not damaged by pornography, they are damaged by a patriarchal culture of which pornography operates as both a symptom and a straw-man for a much more real deep-seated abuse. Many might imagine a sleazy lounge-lizard pornographer in a leopard skin jacket picking up young college girls, dosing them, and getting them on camera (again this scenario is one of violence and abuse and not sex), but I imagine a very genteel man in a suit behind a nice big desk decrying the evils of pornography, birth control, abortion, homosexuals, intellectuals, and terrorists in the same breath.

Finally, pornography is less about the image itself and more about the context of its creation, distribution, viewing and its function as the site of sexual pleasures. Those early grainy tiny images on the web (the moving and moaning version still being popular) are not so much about the image but the viewer partaking of a "risk" activity and imagining themselves as being in the place of the camera (this is their gaze) or camera person (photo fetish).

Ten: Pleasures of the Virtual Body

> *UO* is somewhere I can meet new people and enjoy the company of friends.
> *UO* is where I can fight mythical creatures to the death!
> *UO* is the most exciting virtual space I've ever existed in!
> *UO* is where I've made friends from all over the world!
> *UO* is where I can be a virtuous knight, or an evil, treacherous mage.
> *UO* is the place where I can be whatever I want to be.
>   —Anonymous player quotes from the *Ultima Online* website (c. 1999).

Hundreds of thousands of people from over 114 countries daily log on to online role playing games like *Ever Quest*, *Anarchy Online*, and *The Sims Online*. Many of these gamers come from the traditional RPG and computer game consumer groups made up predominantly of adolescent males. But younger kids play too. And they are not just hanging out online with their older siblings. MMOs have an audience base that includes many adults, and possibly no other venue facilitates the daily interaction between minors and adults than the MMO.

By and large role players are a relatively harmless group, they spend hours poring over bulky manuals, painting figurines, and recording figuring statistics for imaginary creatures. MMOs dispense with the necessity for the geekier activities associated with traditional RPGs—the MMO player needs little more than a computer and access to the internet to log on and play with relatives, friends, and, more often, total strangers.

By combining the technologies of internet chat-rooms and computer video games with the rule systems of traditional RPGs, the designers of MMOs create an impressive array of visual and social environments. But unlike traditional RPGs where the player knows who they are playing with, the average player of an MMO is usually completely ignorant of both the people who run the game and those they play with. The parents of minors are also in the dark.

The modern parent is subjected to incessant warnings about the very real dangers of chat rooms. Children could potentially become the victim of a sexual predator. We are also constantly warned about the possible negative influence of violence in computer games, and though the dangers of RPGs was overstated it was just a few years ago that the condemnation of supposedly satanic RPGs reached a fevered pitch. And yet, no one seems particularly concerned with MMOs. In fact, news stories seem to laud the teenage players who sell their beefed up online accounts as wonder of democracy, free-trade, and individual genius, and entrepreneurship.

I have played online with virtual friends ranging from the ages of 7 to 83. Some are businessmen, some are wives and mothers, quite a few are college students skipping classes and avoiding homework. I even tutored one particularly lackadaisical undergraduate on Shakespeare while our characters drank virtual beer in a virtual pub. MMOs can be very entertaining. They can also be dangerous. One of my characters, a female was subjected to a virtual rape-murder by another player. I watched the tiny body of Ximena (named after my wife) be stabbed repeatedly and "humped" by a virtual little man in a loincloth and skull mask. Though the designers of MMOs have taken great pains to avoid such incidents, they still happen, and verbal abuse is common, as the lengthy Rules of Conduct on most games suggests.

Let's be clear: some person somewhere in the real world made their character assault mine. These are not the computer generated automatons of video games. The great majority of the bodies seen on the screen are controlled by real people, and they could be a teacher, a student, or a child molesting crazy.

The virtual body is already here.

Though not as "seamless" as the virtual body envisioned in cyberpunk literature and made popular in films like *The Lawnmower Man* (1992) and *The Matrix*(1999), hundreds of thousands of people in over 114 countries daily log into online games like *EQ*, *Ultima Online*, *Anarchy Online*, and *The Sims Online*. Games or not, the stakes are high for our body-obsessive culture.

These massively multi-player online role-playing games (MMORPGs or MMOs for short) combine the extensive rule systems of traditional role-playing games (or RPGs) such as *Advanced Dungeons & Dragons* with computer graphic technology and online chat. In these computer generated worlds, players across the world interact with both typed messages and virtual bodies (called the "avatar").

In most cases, the player must choose an avatar from a stock set of bodies and/or body parts. The avatar, which may be more or less detailed depending upon the game, serves as the visual representation of the character within the virtual world and the first line of contact between players. Gone is the brute physical presence of the other players, the bulky manuals piled on the kitchen table, the gem dice of various shapes, and the little lead figurines. The players of MMOs do not need to imagine their characters nor the created world they inhabit: these are supplied for them by the designers of the game. The players of an MMO must imagine each other sitting at a computer somewhere "out there" (if they imagine other players at all).

The importance of the virtual body to these games is highlighted primarily by the centrality of the avatar to character creation. The selection of the avatar (the graphically represented character) is the central activity of character creation; and, in many cases, the group politics of traditional RPGs, where characters are often created in front of other players, gives way to individual choice. Thus, MMOs open the possibility to "cross-dress" online without fear of social repercussions. After all, one player no longer has to "know" that Jack is playing "Galadriel" nor that Jill has created a macho male character named "Killdemall." In fact, the pinnacle, if not the common practice, of good role-playing has always been the player's ability to perform a character very different from her or his own personality and knowledge. In this respect, MMOs do allow the player a range of role-playing potential only dreamed of in traditional RPGs.

Though I began playing *Ultima Online* (*UO*) from a nostalgic impulse to return to my misspent undergraduate years where my friends and I would play *AD&D* for days on end, it never occurred to me to play a female character until my wife, who at that time only watched me play, asked if I had ever tried playing a female. I guiltily created a female character that looked as much like her as possible, named her "Ximena," and headed her off into the woods in search of adventure.

I quickly learned three very important lessons playing a female: first, other players seem particularly interested in your "real" gender; second, other players (especially male) will give you things for free; and third, some men really hate women, even of the virtual variety. Not half an hour after I logged-in to *UO* as a female, a man at the bank was giving me gold (too much for my character to carry), armor (which was too heavy for her to wear), heavy weapons (she couldn't use more than a dagger), food (enough to feed an army), jewelry, and fancy clothing (which have little to no function in the game). I had played a male character for months before and none of this had ever happened. When I played a male, other players were generally nice if I asked a question, but they rarely just "talked" to me, and seldom gave my character anything (though they did occasionally throw things on the ground for any new character to pick up).

The second thing that happened was not quite as pleasant, to say the least: as Ximena was fighting a virtual monster in the woods, another player approached, said "Hi," killed her with a stab in the back, and performed a maneuver over the "dead" avatar which looked for the world like "humping," while "yelling" (accomplished by typing in all caps) very specific obscenities.

I was horrified.

My partner was extremely upset to see her "namesake" assaulted. Suddenly, I had more firsthand knowledge about "being a woman" than I had learned in years of graduate classes in gender studies. My attempted detour into "escapism" landed me smack in the middle of feminist arguments I had spent years trying to understand. Which is not to say that playing a female character online is the same as being a woman (as long as we cling to the rational-humanist subject experiencing the position of the Other will be perpetually outside our grasp) however, nothing but continual and convincing cross-dressing, or becoming a transsexual, gets as close to being the Other as playing in an MMO.

Shortly thereafter, and much to my surprise, the real-life (RL) Ximena began to play *UO* (and, later, other games as well) and together we began to map out the gendered landscape of massively multiplayer online role-playing games. During our play, our characters have been killed by gangs of marauding thugs, received multiple proposals of marriage, gone shopping for clothes to attend dances in virtual nightclubs, and thrown huge parties in virtual houses (with cake and cookies and virtual beer that makes the avatars go *hic*!). And all the while, our characters played virtual "sisters." Other players seem to think we are sisters in real life, and we don't tell them any different.

In the attempt to create games that are more and more "life like" while at the same time allowing freedom of choice for the players, the designers of the MMOs have created a virtual space where a many different fields of human intellectual endeavor come into play. A few of these will seem quite obvious as one cannot well imagine a computer game without implying the computer science (programming and theory) behind it or some type of advertising to sell it, the advertising also implying psychology and sociology and so on. A rapid survey of some of the fields one encounters in an MMO follows, though this list is by no means exhaustive.

Though at this point my intent is primarily descriptive, some fields stand out more clearly than others in the virtual space of the MMO (take, for example, graphic design and cartography) and these will be highlighted where appropriate during the following discussions. Generally, each of these fields may be analyzed on at least three levels of manifestation: 1) the world view within the game, 2) the "external" apparatus actively supporting the virtual world, and 3) the culture that creates the socio-political space for virtual worlds to come into existence and both supports and comments upon them. We might term these Game, Design, and Culture   for short.

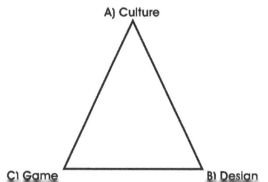

Which one of these would be more accurate and why? The players (and designers) are clearly part of "culture". In the second model, the designers are also "players" for without playing (i.e. running the program) they cannot really understand it to be sure it runs properly.

Computer theorists like to talk of "levels of implementation". For example, if we were to take the ancient discipline of architecture and look at the field of interior design we quite easily find that at the

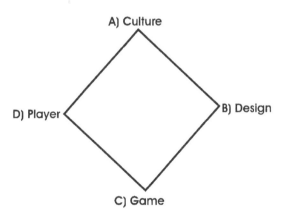

Game-level players interact with interior spaces that have been designed to fit the world-view of the game. In MMOs where house

construction and/or ownership is possible, then the characters can design their own interiors (*Ultima Online* and *The Sims Online* were notable examples here). Notice that I did not use the term "player" in the previous statement as the player would be operating at a different level implementation though clearly interacting with this level as all higher levels of necessity do. Returning to our example, at the Design level of implementation the game designers and programmers must create the programs that set the limits of what may and may not be done in regards to interior design within the virtual world; though as we shall see, the rules they write do not always yield up the expected results as curious and wily players have a tendency to try everything and often reveal what appeared to be a very closed system into a much more open one. But we will get to that later as well. Culturally, of course, we may discuss the history of architecture and interior design all of which create the context for both the Design and Game levels of implementation and is constantly in contact with it. The most important thing to keep in mind here is that each of these levels of implementation are constantly in contact with one another and show a tendency to become increasingly interactive with the Game level effecting both the Design and, eventually, the Culture. Which is not to say that the Game may take over the Culture—by virtue of being at a lower level of implementation, the Game can never fully know what the Design or Culture are doing. However, operating through both the designers (and their corporate proxy) and the players, tropes based in the present cultural context and designed for the game (i.e. a house) work their way back into Culture and modify it. Again, how do we end up with films like *The Game*, *The Matrix*, and *Dungeons and Dragons* to name a few? We may, of course, see these films as an appropriation of a culturally energetic site by Hollywood big business, however, as I argued above, the very fact that these movies are so popular (*Johnny Pneumonic* aside) indicates the cultural interest in the idea of virtuality is gathering force and, thereby, the notice of big business.

The MMO combines the narrative elements of myth, history, and fiction and the temporal-visual elements of film together with real-time interactions with people from around the globe. Like stepping into a movie, the player of the MMO enters a rich, densely populated world with its own set of rules and expectations.

These worlds may be mythical, historical, fantastical, or futuristic (SF Anarchy Online), or real-life simulation (TSO). By far the most popular to date have been the fantasy games like *Ultima Online* and *Everquest*, but this fact most likely has more to do with the history of games and gaming culture than anything inherent in the media. The quick success of *The Sims Online* for example (notwithstanding its early demise), heralds a new era of the of the RPG and MMO–an era where none of us can help but be affected by the new virtual culture.

Where the player of a traditional RPG sits and imagines her character—what she must look like, what she was wearing—existing in a world spun in word by the DM or GM, the player of the MMO *sees* the visual representation of the made world on-screen and, therefore, must try to imagine the player. I can now see what the character looks like—I can see the avatar and only the avatar—and am left only to wonder about the player.

One effect of this distancing of players is that MMOs create a context where players can explore sex and gender differences by performing all genders without fear of direct censure from other players. No one is going to make fun of me if I choose to play a female as long as I play the role effectively; and even if they do so *in game* the psychological impact is much less than a direct face-to-face confrontation. That not all players choose to perform another gender, nor necessarily enjoy the experience when they do, does not negate the fact that never before have we had such an open and, at least on the surface, risk-free chance to experiment with the performance of other bodies and genders. In MMOs we can all do a little drag.

The fact that players are invited to select a body (rather than being assigned one based on their RL sex) re-envisions "sex" as a possible "choice" rather than a biological fact. Likewise, the necessity for a verbal construction of gender (regardless of the avatar's gender) further undermines the notion of the physical body as the origin of gender: a female player can play a male character without any attempt to conceal her real world gender and thus be treated as a female regardless of the physical evidence supplied by the avatar. These cross-gendered performances highlight the performative nature of sex and gender, ultimately opening it to critique with a wider audience than could have been possible before. This potential for "casual cross-dressing"—or even interacting with the casual cross dressers—of a segment of our community clearly has the potential for a wider ranging social impact. After all, in the end, we are the roles we play.

MMOs may further interrogate our notion of a unified body, a single physical unit, which contains the self. The body of the player comes into play through the fingers clicking the keys, the ears listening to the music and straining for the telltale approach of monsters, the eyes scanning the screen, the back that arching from too much sitting, all reminding us that we have another body somewhere "out here." The feeling of hunger (weakness and growling stomach) is replaced with a visual input in the form of text "You are feeling very hungry" or graphic percentage (a declining bar of "stamina"). Satisfaction comes in the form of increased percentages, textual congratulations for treating your body well, and better performance. The fact that players can feel disembodied (out of full control, hitting the wrong button, etc.) implies that they can feel *embodied* while playing. As one player described the experience, "You have this intensely nagging feeling that *your body* is not working." Soon, we may all have the nagging feeling that our bodies do not mean what they used to either. Now I actually inhabit the Venus of Willendorf every day—or at least her daughter's, daughter's, daughter.

Massively-multiplayer online role-playing games (MMORPGs or MMOs for short)[31] developed from the strange juxtaposition of

---

[31] MMORPG is quite possibly the worst acronym in history. It reads like a city name in a Terry Pratchett novel. Many of these games are also Persistent State Worlds (meaning the game is not dependent on any one player or sets of players). Thankfully, no one to my knowledge has yet suggested the acronym MMORPGPSW.

war games, traditional role-playing games, video games, and internet email and chat. Role-playing games have always been a fringe sort of affair freely associated with geek culture, satanic rituals, drug culture, heavy metal music, tattoos, and piercings. But they also have a long and distinguished history in the development of civilization and the expansion of humanity over the globe—if, that is, one considers the history of humanity at war to be a "distinguished history.

In a traditional RPG, a player might miss a gaming session, but otherwise, the fantasy world did not go on without them. The same is true of the computer games; shut the game down and nothing happens until you logon again. In the case of MMOs, the world is a persistent state world. generally speaking, the game goes on with or without individual players. In essence the game does not revolve around the group of players but around the world itself.

In the traditional RPG players typically know their own statistics and may learn the statistics that govern the world at large. Generally, however, only the GM knows all the numerical bases for the particular adventure and this adds to the enjoyment of the game and makes it seem less artificial and more real. In the MMO, however, players may not even know their own statistics or the numerical bases for their characters. Though the virtual world runs on numerical values (and being based in computer programs, is more closely restricted to those numbers) the players do not know the statistics for the world (and for a variety of reasons, MMO designers keep these close to the belt). Perhaps one of the most realistic elements of UO was the fact that players never knew exactly how many experience points they had.

Starting a new character in an MMO can be a highly confusing affair. Generally, the player must negotiate several screens where she or he must choose the character they would like to create from a wide variety of options. These choices include some combination of profession, base physical and mental attributes, species and/or race, gender, equipment, clothing, political and/or religious affiliation, and "home town." The ability of the character to perform *any* function is based on physical and mental *attributes*. Attributes are the virtual body rendered in quantifiable (numerical) form. Attributes are often based on the *Dungeons & Dragons* model of Strength, Intelligence, Wisdom, Dexterity and Charisma with modifications appropriate to the particular setting: a science fiction game, for example, may want to include a "psionic" attribute so players can utilize ESP-like abilities. The attributes make up the "body" of the character in its expression through actions. Though we may not see a physical difference of size, for example, between two avatars on the screen, one character's ability to bust open a door or wear heavy armor defines the character as being physically stronger. Players often boast about how strong (or smart, or quick, etc.) their characters are by using the actual number value. Physical attributes in the games are strictly objectified in a way that is not possible in the outside world. Some games allow different minimum and maximum attributes based on gender. Females may be, in general, not as strong as males, but they are quicker. Game designers argue that they merely wish to make the rules of the game fit as closely as possible to the observed world where the strongest man in our world is (currently) physically stronger than the strongest woman even though some women are stronger than most men. Of course, they seem to forget that magic does not work in the observed world and elves are a myth. Therefore, they merely uncritically replicate the cultural norms where physical strength is defined by traditional "feats of strength" based on the performance of the male body. These are political narratives of the body and either reinforce or question stereotypes.

It is understandable then, that many players go through lots of "test characters" before they fully understand the choices and find a character that suits their style of play. Despite their differences, however, all MMOs, make the choice of the avatar and its appearance (and thereby the virtual gender of the character) a central concern. Some of these choices have both a numerical and visual value. For example, "comeliness" (or "attractiveness") may have a numerical value, say 60/100, which affects character interaction with non-player characters (NPCs). The NPC shopkeeper might sell their products cheaper to a "pretty" woman or give them more information than a less attractive character. Visually, however, other players might not be inclined to agree with the numerical assessment and might choose to ignore it altogether. In traditional RPGs, it was technically not possible to "ignore" the statistic: the Game Master (GM) or Dungeon Master (DM) was supposed to give the "pretty" player a statistical chance of using their looks to convince other players to have their characters do something they were not particularly inclined to do otherwise.

In a sense, then, characters in MMOs have two bodies, the numerical and the graphic (what I am terming the "character" and "avatar"), which may be more or less in accord with one another. Thus, I may have a character who does not "match" with the visual representation. Further, the character probably does not "match" with my own abilities. I may have a character who is extremely stupid numerically (an I.Q. equivalent of "moronic") who, nevertheless, is not role-played that way. For example, in *UO*, I play a character who is extremely unintelligent, having chosen to "spend points" on strength and dexterity instead. Her only restriction, however, is that she cannot use magic well. In this case, I have chosen to read "intelligence" as a skill rather than an actual I.Q. In fact, it is entirely possible in *UO* to "become smarter," but at the sake of other attributes.

This multiform (player, character, avatar) "variable body" questions the "fact" of biological deterministic narratives. Ultimately, the obsession with defining the body—how strong, how fast, how smart, how attractive—becomes in MMOs highly voyeuristic as players choose from the body options available to "build" a graphically represented body. In the *UO* character creation screens, for example, the choice of gender for the character is limited, predictably, to male and female. The male, appearing first on the screen, is the "base" choice—woman is the "other" choice indicating that the world is male unless otherwise specified. All bodies of the same gender are structurally identical, and it is not possible to change the face nor body shape or size. Hairstyle and skin tone are the only options for the base avatar beyond gender.

Variation is possible, however: my wife created a short-haired Negroid female by mixing a female body with "receding" blonde hairstyle and darkening the avatar's skin to a deep brown. Her racial performance is often commented upon (positively and negatively) by other characters in the game, a *very* few of whom have also constructed a "black" avatar. Though some of the hairstyles seem more appropriate to one gender or the other, both genders may choose from the same list. These choices include curly (which looks not a little like Don King), completely bald, two tails, long, "Princess Leia" double buns, and a receding style (actually a widow's peak). Male avatars, however, do have the additional choice of several styles of facial hair, and the accompanying choice of hair color, that gives them more body range.[32] Though a minor point, perhaps, I feel I must point out that the male, as usual, has to have that "little extra"—a difference by addition. After all, the female avatar does not have an equivalent secondary sex characteristic such as breast size and shape for example. One could argue that secondary sex characteristics for the female avatars are omitted because they are already there (the women *do* have breasts), or they are omitted because parents would view these choice as too erotic (or facial hair is a real-world choice for men and not women). All three cases, however, highlight an inherent societal misogyny expressed in the game. In the first case, the designers choose the "perfect" form in deciding appropriate breast size; in the second case the designers ignore the fact that bras which "lift and separate" or otherwise alter breast size and shape are widely available and visible in every shopping mall and department store (not to mention surgical alterations); and finally, the designers' inclusion of the choice of beard, with no equivalent choice for the female, merely serves to give the avatar an additional outward symbol of virility.

Additionally, the player may initially express the avatar's individuality through the choice of a color scheme for their clothing, though "newbie gear" is quickly disposed of in the game. The very

---

[32] This is in some way compensated by the availability of "female armor" which only women can wear.

fact that this choice exists, and in such a wide variety (there are as many color choices for clothing as for the more permanent hair and skin color), belies the importance of outward expressions of personality in the game. Thus, the most essential choice in creating a character in *UO*, the choice which can never be changed for that character, is gender, while at the same time, gender is solely a social designation as no skills or attributes in *UO* are gender specific.

In contrast to the minimal, almost unisex approach of *UO*, *EverQuest* (EQ) offers the full range of fantasy race favorites. The current species at this writing included Human, Barbarian (a large, thick-hipped humanoid), Dwarf, Gnome, High Elf (a species apparently descended from Nordic models), Wood Elf, Half-elf, Erudite (a magical Negroid species), Iksar (a reptilian species), Trolls (whose females wear bark bikinis), Ogres, and Vah Shir (a feline species).[33] *EQ* overtly fetishizes the body by playing on fantasy art representations of voluptuous babes in skimpy, push-up amour and muscle-bound loin-cloth wearing men.[34] The extensive selection of races does, however, allow a broad spectrum of choice in body styles. The ability to additionally choose faces (also from a finite list) gives the avatar an individual body look.[35] One quickly learns in-game, however, that what seems like a wide variety of choices is actually minimal considering the number of players in the game and the popularity of some "looks". After just a few weeks of play, all the faces are easily recognizable and players begin to rely on other indicators of individuality, most commonly the visible name or some identifying color scheme or rare piece of clothing. Perhaps most telling about the character creation screen is the high-tech voyeuristic performance of the avatar. Like a stripper on a spinning stage, the bodies "perform" for the player while rotating to

---

[33] *EQ* adds new species as part of their regular expansions.

[34] The use of "babe art" is prolific and based in the "tradition" of RPG and SF/F fandom. Virtually all of *EQ*'s promotions feature the "EverQuest babe": a blonde haired, fair-skinned elfish woman.

[35] Likewise, Microsoft's amazingly playable *Asheron's Call* featured a standardized body for both the male and the female which was large (for both sexes) and "athletic looking." The choice of not only faces, but actual features (noses, eyes, hairstyles, even scars) makes the avatar even more individualistic.

afford the 360-degree view. Players "check out" different faces until they find the body and face combination they are interested in playing in-game. The fact that only those who purchase the regular updates have full access to all the bodies shown further emphasizes the impression that the player is "buying" bodies, or at least body options. In *EverQuest*, while the choice of gender is subsumed to the choice of species, gender choice does have an effect on the character beyond the appearance of the avatar: males and females of all species have different attributes (women characters, in general, are not as strong as men, etc.). Combined with the game's tendency towards large-breasted, leggy females in skimpy clothing, *EQ* clearly adheres more closely to the traditional RPG attitude of "by men for men" about which many women computer gamers complain.[36]

The science fiction MMO *Anarchy Online* (*AO*) offers the most interesting, and non-traditional, variety of body styles. Players start with a "genderless clone" whose body they supposedly "inhabit" and which is replaced with an identical copy after each "death" (strangely implying that the player, and not the character, is the soul). The player must then choose from the available four humanoid "breeds" to imprint on their clone body. To date, *AO* is the only game to work the choice of the virtual body (character creation) into the narrative of the game by adding an explanation for the necessity to choose a body: only your "soul" is sent to the new planet. In *AO* the choice of "body" is worked into the narrative of the game. New characters are "colonists" who will be implanted into a clone body which then, due to local regulations and "corporate policy" must choose a body type and political allegiance. Microsoft's *Asheron's Call* does make some attempt to explain the presence of the avatar in a "foreign land" (magical space travel), but does not incorporate the choice of body into the narrative. While clearly supporting the mind/body dichotomy by positing the "self"

---

[36] See, for example, Cornelia Brunner, Dorothy Bennet, and Margaret Honey, "Girl Games and Technological Desire," *Barbie to Mortal Kombat: Gender and Computer Games*. Ed. Justine Cassell and Henry Jenkins. Cambridge, MA: MIT Press, 1999.

as independent from the body, *AO* also pastiches its own generic conventions: the "colonist" has to choose a body adapted to the world of the colony just as the player must choose an avatar to enter the virtual world. Thus, the line between player and character is blurred as the game posits the *player* as the *character*.[37]

The available races in *AO* included Homo-solitus (a genetically altered hyper human who serves as the "norm" for the other breeds), the smaller punk-elf Homo-opifex, a cyborg breed called Homo-nano, and the Homo-atrox, a supposed epicene (genderless) breed. The Atrox ("designed" as a mine-worker) has a reduced mental capacity and no reproductive capabilities due to genetic manipulation and an excess of steroids. The possibilities for exploring gender and body issues in this context are innumerable. The science-fiction narrative allows the designers to support a narrative of evolutionary technology (through cloning and genetic manipulation) while at the same time questioning such technology in the internal politics of the game: it is a well-known "secret" divulged in the manual that the colonizing corporation Omni-tek has produced monstrous "accidents" which are loose in the world.[38] The inclusion of the epicene breed, Atrox, also begs questions of sex and gender. Why do the designers use the word "gender" for the Atrox instead of "sex"?[39] What is a "virtual sex"? As none of the avatars can really reproduce (virtual babies are not yet an option), what does it mean that the Atrox is labeled as such? Why does the first "genderless" being in a game look like a Nordic, male, bodybuilder gone whacky on steroids? The implied joke here on steroids and impotency (and even loss of reproductive organs) belies a

---

[37] It is also possible that players take the "your" in "your mind" to refer to the character and not the player. However, the direct address in the manual and the game creates the context (unlike other games) where the player may feel a part of the narrative.

[38] In fact, most of the monsters encountered are defined as one type of genetic "mistake" or another.

[39] The most obvious answer is that they wished to avoid even the use of the word as the primary target audience for these games is the U.S., though other countries— notably Japan, Australia, France, and Germany—are rapidly gaining on U.S. playership.

preoccupation with sex and gender issues and makes *AO* the most gender-conscious, one might even say body-obsessive, of the games currently playable online. *AO* further fetishizes the body by giving the player the choice of multiple faces and hairstyles, which cover a wide variety of races in the Solitus breed. The player must also choose the avatar's "Percent Body Fat" (ranging from painfully thin to fat) and height (10% taller or shorter than normal for the breed), making *AO* one of the most advanced in terms of body diversity.

The number of body styles available to players will only increase as improved technology allows for faster internet connections and larger, faster servers to run the programs. For example, *Earth and Beyond* (EB), a science-fiction space exploration game, provided a very wide range of body styles; however, EB also has the lowest use of the avatar as a great deal of play time is spent in a personal spaceship, thus the advanced body forms do not take up as much memory as few characters are using them at any given time. As we will see in the next section, however, the choice of the virtual body may be essential to the creation of a character, but *how* that body is played—how gender is performed within the context of world of the game—offers the greatest opportunity for examining the cultural construction of the gendered body.

The design of the quantified character supports a particular narrative of the body. Skills that are primary to class suggest that the physical body including mental abilities is the essential element of personhood. Likewise narratives that posit race as the defining characteristic of the virtual subject support cultural narratives of essential racial differences. Narratives based on class however imply that we are rather the work we perform, that our bodies are changed by the work we do. Once within the game however attributes grow and change. But the initial choice gives the player the sense that this is the most important choice in the game and in fact it is. The choice of the virtual self will, for the most part, set the limits for the player in the game. This of course is one explanation for why most players go through a number of characters before settling on one and why many players consistently play more than one character.

An interesting manifestation of this ability to play multiple characters (though multiple accounts are required to play them at the same time) is the creation of so-called mule characters whose primary function is to use their skills to support other more specialized characters. An example might include a character who chops wood and makes arrows for a higher level archer character or a character with blacksmith abilities to make and repair armor for a warrior or a trader to get good deals on items and the most money for the sale of found items.

These multiple bodies may be understood by the player as employees of sorts and yet the player still must perform all of the characters and this cannot but have some impact on the players conception of their own bodies and sense of personhood. It is certainly no coincidence that films like *The Matrix* are so popular.

Playing an MMO for the first time can be a bewildering experience. Like a newborn, new players must literally learn how to walk by properly manipulating the keys and controls. Of course, playing an MMO is complicated by the fact that many of the other "people" you see are other players rather than computer-controlled non-player characters (NPCs), which populate traditional computer RPGs like the *Might and Magic* series. In fact, the new player can be easily overwhelmed by the sheer number of people and level of activity.[40] There are even several online comic strips devoted to the misadventures of characters in these virtual environments who never quite "get it" though they try really hard. One of the most well-known, the *UO* comic *Ima-Newbie*,[41] chronicles the exploits of Ima as he blunders his way around Britannia. One of the ongoing storylines in *Ima Newbie* is his on again off again love affair with

---

[40] Some games have newbie training programs or newbie areas. For example *EQ* comes with a training program which operates off line while *Ultima Online* has a training city and a "safer" world to begin in where no player versus player is possible.

[41] Available at http://www.imanewbie.com.

Irma Dufus. That the strip features "dating" as a major theme echoes in parody players' in-game experience of virtual relationships.

All of which highlights the fact that playing an online character is not easy. In fact, I would suggest that playing an online character well is like playing Jazz piano well—improvisation is the key to the keys and the you don't have time to think at all or hunt down every keystroke—you just have to *know* and the avatar acts like the piano sounds.[42] "Newbies" (new players) move erratically, running into walls, or stand, frozen in place, as they hysterically search the manual for the proper keystrokes which allow them to "speak" to other characters, and they may be trapped "in-game," unable to find the exit command.

Actual body movement of the avatar ranges from simple walking (usually holding down an arrow key or pointing the mouse) to more complex series of actions sometimes programmable by the player. The wider range of motion creates the possibility for more complex, and even transgressive, body performances. In *UO*, the first and least visually complex of the MMOs, avatars have been able to "bow" since the game first hit the shelves. Players, however, quickly adapted bowing into a wider range of motion including barfing, sneezing, "head-banging," and the aforementioned "humping." Other games (including *EQ*, *Asheron's Call* [*AC*], and *Ultima Online 3D*) have a wide range of social actions including various forms of waving, cheering, laughing, and dancing. Some of these motions are clearly comical such as "the chicken dance" (*AO*) and "I'm a little teapot" (*AC*). *AO* currently has the longest list of social moves including several pre-scripted dance styles that can be combined in a plethora of ways to produce highly individualistic dances.

I once saw a virtual table dancer performing for a group of male avatars who were "tipping" her in game currency. In none of the games currently online in 2002 was true nudity possible, though one could easily find a program for *The Sims Online* that removes the

---

[42] I am indebted to Paul Connerton's book *How Societies Remember* (Cambridge, UK: Cambridge UP, 1989) for this conceit.

"fuzzy bar" from over the undressed avatar and *Neocron* did have what appear to be nude strippers, though they were about as detailed as a Barbie Doll. Now, however, "adult" environments allow nudity but cannot be considered a "game" by the definition used here. Revealing clothing, however, is another matter altogether, and *AO* boasts the largest selection of clothes including lingerie. The performance was created by interweaving a variety of social-moves including a "supplication" (inexplicably called the "apache") combined with a "spin" to shake the avatar's bottom in the other avatars' faces. When one of the male players became rude, she pulled a very large machine gun and pointed it at him, apparently out of nowhere. (The character generally has a storage space that is not visible on the avatar. This space, which can hold quite a few items, allows for the possibility of an apparently unarmed body to conceal a small arsenal "somewhere inside." This invisible, impossible space is one of the zones of interchange between the character and the avatar. One occasionally hears a player comment on this effect as "pulling it out of your ass.") While obviously a fetish performance, the simulated stripping may actually expose the performance it simulates: this is not a real strip bar, nor a real stripper, nor maybe even a "real" girl (player). Further, that the performance appears in the game at all illustrates some awareness that the strip club in real life is also a "game" enacted ultimately by men (owners) for men (customers) with the female body as the means of exchange. The entrance of the phallic performance further highlights the actual exchange: as long as the male characters play the game properly, "she" will hide her phallus (the large machine gun) from them.

Physical motions and outward expressions of the body are, however, still limited even in the most progressive games. It is not possible, for example, for the avatar to smile, or wink, or even blink: though the now defunct *Earth and Beyond* incorporated avatars who "breathe" even when at rest and which are capable of "moods" such as happy or angry indicated by an alteration in the avatar's facial features. Players overcome the physical limitation of the avatar by using emotes.

Emotes, verbal expressions of the virtual body inherited from chat rooms, are usually differentiated from speech-text by enclosing asterisks. Thus, for example, though the avatar cannot shrug its shoulders, the player can type *shrugs shoulders* or *shrugs* to give the impression of a bodily action. The range of emotes is only limited to the player's vocabulary and imagination. Some emotes are standardized across the virtual community such as LOL (laughs out loud), ROFL (rolling on the floor laughing), and its extension ROFLMAO (rolling on the floor laughing my ass off). Even in games like *AO* where social moves are frequent, emotes still play a large role in diversifying "bodily" expressions.

The virtual body has a certain self-similar grace, that perfect form of the professional runner. This very perfection is the limiting factor, however, for unlike the dancer whose individuality is lost to the dance as they surpass skill and move farther into the faceless music, the avatar can never succeed its programming and perfection. And yet we might argue that sameness is a true expression of our own state, or an expression of what we fear-that we are all the same, and what truly defines us are trinkets, baubles, and adornments.

The senses in the virtual world are reduced from five to two— sight, sound, smell, taste, and touch are all collapsed into the visual and the aural. And yet, this is not quite true for the meat body does not cease to exist and continues to receive input: fingers still grace the keyboard, the hand moves the mouse, the eyes burn and the back aches. I laugh out loud even as I type "LOL"—though I do not roll on the floor as often as I type "ROFL" and have rarely, if ever, laughed my ass off, "LMAO".

Due to the importance of the avatar in social communication, MMOs tend to have a complex system of body modifications to further individualize the virtual body. The most common modifications to the avatar are social and protective body coverings. These are typically items of clothing and armor, which may or may not offer some factor of protection as well. For example, *UO* offers a wide range of armor and clothing types, many of which may be dyed a wide variety of colors by the players themselves. *AO* even has a virtual haute couture fashion line that sells expensive, designer clothing in retail outlets. Other "perks" include hair dyes in a wide range of colors that include neon pink and purple and blue (*UO*), hairstyle changes *(UO)*, masks (*EverQuest* and *UO*), designer sunglasses (*AO*), and body tattoos (*AO*). Thus, money buys individuality: the more virtual money the character has, the more the player can individualize the avatar.[43]

That all that precious memory space is expended on clothes and less on individualizing the bodies indicates that, while the creation of the avatar is certainly pleasurable, the longer term pleasure lies not in that body alone, but in the expression of individuality through acquisition. In many games this fact is accentuated by "name brand" clothing equivalents that look identical to the more common varieties and have no special attributes other than a bit of text describing them as "Designs by Mir" or "Golden Armor by Wolfenstien." These items are much sought out and as much for their personalizing powers as for any protective quality (indeed many items have absolutely no practical function beyond their appearance).

This is a world view based in the notion that we are all basically the same in body and that which differentiates the majority of us from another is not so much a matter of biology as of finances and matters of taste.

We might easily label this world view the GQ-Vogue Complex. In these magazines the models certainly do look remarkably alike physically (as do avatars in the MMOs). Indeed, few are truly memorable at all beyond the generic designation of "model." In matters of physical appearance, one is a good as another.

Thankfully, the long slender arm of the fashion model mafia does not often reach across the East River into Queens, so I should be safe enough that twiggy lot to write as I wish. Though, I will not soon be invited to a fashion show, I fear. Well, so be it. My subject matter is virtual reality and fashion models certainly know all about

---

[43] The virtual currency even has a real world value as it is exchanged for real currency on websites such as *ebay*.

that. Their collective bodies are nodes of gathering power for technologies of the body.

I do not wish to deconstruct the fashion industry here, and there is very little to deconstruct built as it is on fabric and air merely draped on flesh and bone, but the performance itself is noteworthy as the models are bodies performing bodies. They permeate the media and exceptional bodies become quite the norm and the normal is seen as exceptional. Yes, there is yet another role the body must play--that of being too fat. How can we say our bodies are solid when they so clearly change from day to day in our own and others eyes.

This is the truth that MMOs tell us about our bodies and fashion: within certain definable categories, our bodies look pretty much the same. Check any Introduction to Anthropology textbook, or human biology, or nursing and you will see the types delineated there for review.

In-game chat, or textual "speech," is the main indicator of the character's virtual gender and, by extension, the player's gender as well. The chat generally takes one or more of the following forms: over the head speech, a chat window, or an external chat service (like IM or ICQ). In game, it is possible to "whisper" and "shout" changing the range of your "voice" to include all those in a broad area or only the character leaning in to your virtual ear. Players can be highly creative in their "verbal" performance, establishing a clear, virtual personality for their character. Shibboleths abound as well: the best known example being the so-called "KoOL duDEs" who randomize capital and lower case letters and have alternate spellings of many words. Their association with a group is further marked by the sameness in their dress. In the case of *UO* they wear gray death shrouds and "skeleton helms." Another, less well known group is O.R.C. whose members wear Orc masks (a humanoid derived from Tolkien's *Lord of the Rings*), Orc armor, and "perform" the "monster" of their title by speaking "like an Orc" (replicating the programmed speech of said monster).

In my own case, each of my more developed characters has a unique speech pattern filled with it's (though I am tempted to say "his or her") own speech artifacts—many of which I have never used out of the game. For example, one of my characters often greets other characters with "Hiya," an expression I have never used at any other time. The same character also uses the words "cutie" and "sweetie"—as in "you're such a cutie"—almost obsessively. These examples of "trademark speech" help define the persona of the online character, and no doubt lead to the conclusion on the part of other players that I, the player, am a female. In this case, I am mimicking my perception of female speech (and, at times, of an admittedly stereotypical variety). But after three years of playing the same character, can we say that I am still *consciously* mimicking the feminine? Or, is it possible that the character "Ximena" is truly gendered female despite my (the player's) gender? If the character "talks like a male," the player is assumed to be male. If the character "talks like a female," the player is assumed to be a female. Though there is an undercurrent of fear regarding the "cross-dressing" player, most players will apparently believe another player's proffered gender—but only insofar as the character's gender performance meets expectations.

Occasionally, a player goes out of her/his way to explain that she/he is "really" one gender or another. Take, for example, the case of the character Nadia. Dressed in a matching pink beret and skirt with a white puffy top, Nadia stands by the bank in a major *UO* town. Opening her information sheet, however, reveals the following text: "I know this is why you are looking at my profile, so no, I'm not really a female." This player's "confession" highlights not only "his" desire to avoid awkward speech with other male players, but also a more complex relationship between player and character. As "he" explains, "Nadia is the only female character on my account and by far the most enjoyable to play. It just happens that when I made this character, I had not intended to use her as one of my main characters."[44] The confession (of the player's supposed gender) is thus followed by an apology for the cross-gendered performance (it wasn't intentional), while at the same time it justifies that performance (it is enjoyable). What, exactly, is the source of the player's enjoyment of the performance of the female avatar? Obviously the "enjoyment" does not come from the gendered performance itself as the "confession" is presumably intended to ward off online suitors, and further to avoid answering the question "Are you a girl in RL?" repeatedly. But, the player *does* dress Nadia in a very "feminine," and one might say, nicely attractive, way indicating that some of the "enjoyment" is centered in the cross-gendered body performance.

---

[44] Again, I am taking the player's expression of real-world gender at face value as the address is clearly coded as "player to player."

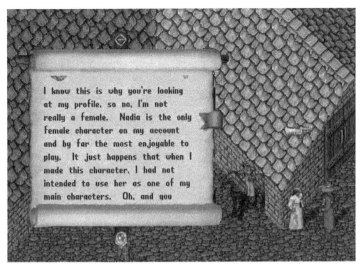

While we could focus on the voyeuristic elements of the performance highlighting the player's "ownership" of the female character/avatar as the base for the player's enjoyment (noting how he highlights that he "made her") we might also indicate the player's own *performance* of Nadia as gender transgressive, regardless of his confession. After all, if one does not check the profile, nor ask for the player's gender, this individual does otherwise attempt to role-play Nadia as a female.

According to French philosopher Michel Foucault, the confession 1) assumes an authority (even if it be a virtual one) who can meet out justice, forgiveness, consolation, punishment, etc.; 2) the very difficulty of the confession (in this case "I am not a girl in RL" yet also "But I enjoy playing Nadia) serves to verify its truthfulness, and the more difficult the confession is the more true it is; 3) the person is changed by the confession, made clean, whole, and so on. What is interesting about the Nadia case is that while the confession seems necessary, assuming the higher power/authority of the social norm (i.e. to not confess, to fully play the girl would be to engage in a bodily falsehood, to lie about one's sex, to be gay or transsexual) Nadia confession does not seem particularly difficult and yet still true. We can only surmise that the confession then is a pre-emptive measure to cut off the possibility of a future pain brought on by the question "Are you a girl in RL?" This is rather like a transvestite who wears a beard or a shirt proclaiming "I am not really a girl," though not a shirt proclaiming "I am not a transvestite." Perhaps Nadia's pleasure is located both in the performance and the confession, or the image and the confession. Either way, "Nadia" is in a continual state of transgression and confession.

Certainly the compulsion to confess comes not from a manifest authority. The rules of the game suggest this type of behavior, this confession, is unnecessary and may disrupt other players' enjoyment of the game. In fact to continually break the rules of role-playing, to "stay in character," evidences adherence to a deeper, faceless authority that, as Foucault suggest, comes "from below".[45]

Compare Nadia's profile with another character, appropriately named Jaded: "HEeyyyy my name is Rochelle [row-shell] What's up? ya I'm a girl gamer and u better believe it! boys suck ok? ya ....hmm if you would like to icq me my # is 22723150 wooo!" Unlike Nadia, Jaded is dressed in only thigh-high boots and jewelry (the "underwear bikini" is standard). Further, she has a guild title, which proclaims her as "Playboy Bunny, COD." In this case, the inclusion of the player's supposed name, Rochelle, the correct pronunciation

---

[45] Foucault, *History of Sexuality: Part I* (62).

(even though "speaking" is not possible per se) and the indication that "boys suck" are all offered as evidence of the player's female gender. Further, Jaded's style of speech is typical of the "game grrlz" movement: female gamers with "in your face attitude" and (nominally) 21st century feminist opinions who enjoy beating men at their own (computer) games.[46] The performance of Jaded is not atypical. Some female players apparently prefer to play the "sexy female" role. However, these players have received much flak from other female players who see their behavior as a serious threat to the goal of eliminating stereotypes within the gaming industry and gaming culture.

All of these instances would seem to support the notion of an essential gender as most players do not believe that a player can sustain the role of a character of another gender for any length of time. However, considering my own experiences in playing MMOs and countless of hours of interaction with thousands of other players, I believe these complex "body" performances may result in the following: 1) a strong identification between player and a particular avatar, 2) an increased tendency for the player to view the avatar as a "person" in its own right, 3) an increased tendency for other players to view the avatar as a "person" in its own right, 4) an increased tendency for other players to think the avatar is a "true" physical manifestation of the player, and at the extreme, 5) the notion of a true, sexed body might be undermined. The same way that teenagers are presumably numbed to violence through television, alternate body styles and gender options may eventually become the societal "norm" due in part to the virtual performance of "other" bodies.

---

[46] See, for example, Henry Jenkins "Combat Zone: Game Grrlz Talk Back," in *From Barbie to Mortal Kombat: Gender and Computer Games.*

Another issue in the case of *AO* is the gendered difference in some of the body moves. Both males and females can dance "Disco," for example, but perform it differently (women dance "The Hustle" and men the "*Saturday Night Fever*"). Notably, the Atrox have dance versions of the gendered moves that support a body narrative not entirely based on the two-gender model.

Some games, of course, are more mature than others. By far the one game that carries the greatest potential for adult themes and encounters is *The Sims Online*. Based on *The Sims* computer game series that began with *Sim City*, *The Sims Online* takes the immensely popular home-based virtual family game and recreates it as an MMO. While many parents may see little harm in their children playing virtual house in the privacy of their own home, few would like their 12 year old daughter to engage in virtual marriage or virtual sex with a 37 year old car salesman in Duluth.

Admittedly, like most MMOs, *The Sims Online* clearly warns of "adult content" on the package: the game is labeled "Mature." When *Ultima Online* first came out, the grown-up credit card it used to take to play an MMO. However, the addition of the gaming card (or pre-paid play time card), broadening the market to include purchasers who use only cash and those who would like to control their children's play time, can be purchased through any gaming store without an ID check. One more barrier between the kids and the virtual world bites the dust.

All intent from the designers of *The Sims Online* aside, the rules of the game focus on three primary goals—making friends and connections, making money, and satisfying desires. The virtual "escorts" make friends, satisfy their own programmed desires, and make money while doing it. In a game where frequent physical contact is necessary, virtual "sex" is possible, and doorways can have a toll put on them, the virtual brothel was inevitable.

Ultimately, the virtual world is a mature world with at least some of the problems of this one. Adult players should realize the effect their play has on their own body image. Parents should treat a visit to on online world as a trip away from home—is your child old enough to go it alone?

Everyone who plays MMOs regularly has at least one tale of online love. The primary draws of the MMO has always been social interaction as everything else about the MMO is inferior to the video game and computer game. MMOs are smaller, slower, have less detailed graphics, and are not always available to play. Like its ancestor the chat-room, online games are an airing house of politics and opinions. Though some gamers try to remain "in character," the great majority of the players will freely chat about the game, their lives, where they live, what school they go to (or teach at) and what their favorite movie is.

Conversation quickly turns personal as players ask of female characters "Are you a girl in RL (real life)"? They usually have no choice but to take the "yes or no" at face value. Players frequently make "dates" to meet online to play, hang out, and chat, all with people they have never actually met. But, unlike the chat-room, players in an MMO can also send their characters on an in-game date complete with dinner, music, and a moonlit boat ride.

More intimate contact is accomplished through chat emotes such as *hug,* *slow dance,* and *kiss* (the asterisks signifying an action). Now, however, several games have worked "social actions" into the game and players can watch as their characters perform any number gestures including dancing in several styles, laughing, drinking, eating, and waving goodbye. (Some of the social moves are less than polite, such as *Anarchy Online*'s "finger," and "mooning" and *The Sims Online* "fart.")

Not only do players have their characters flirt and date, most of the games have rules for "in-game" marriages where the two characters (and not the players) are married by one of the game officials. These marriages are not in any way binding even within the game, but players often spend months planning these virtual events by buying special cakes, wedding dresses, brides maid dresses, and picking the right location (all virtual) not to mention getting everyone on line at the same time. The guest list can number in the hundreds for some couples. The emotional investment can run very high.

More than a few online marriages have been legally binding, however, as the bride, the groom, and the marrying official were all in the same room and logged into the game at the same time. The actual wedding was performed in the game for all their online friends to see. Online marriages of the less legal variety set no requirements on the ages of the players themselves

This virtual body changes the way we see our flesh body just as cinema, TV, and print media and advertising. One primary difference, however, is the active experience the player has with the virtual body. Not only have they designed and dressed the avatar, but the physically interact with it with the eyes, ears, and fingers— the main difference, of course, is the fingers, the body, and the ability to control the image of the virtual body. But what sense of embodiment does one get from continual online play?

Just as the regular participant in a chat room might begin to feel as if they know someone well after only the briefest of online encounters--somehow the written words on the screen create a discursive space large enough to hold all the desires of the other without physical contact—so, too, the avatar allows ego projection. And yet, the avatar body gives this discursive space a visual limit.

The pleasure associated with the performance of the virtual body takes several forms. First we have the visual pleasure of gazing at this created body. As the forms of the avatar are defined by the design teams—still mostly made up of men--the avatar generally takes on predictable characteristics of culturally defined notions of beauty. Many of the bodies one sees in these environments are atypical, unlikely, or impossible. We might think of the waspish form of Laura Croft, for example. But there is also a visual pleasure in forms traditionally considered as unattractive or grotesque such as heavy and even non-human forms. In both cases players typically take pleasure in the display of the virtual form. One player, an acquaintance of mine and regular game player on the more traditional offline video platform created a female character and was fascinated with her buttocks in motions. Now we might say this is also true of virtual girls like Virtual Valerie and Laura Croft, however two distinct differences immediately presented themselves: my friend began directly to refer to said posterior in the first person "look at my ass," he said and, "I have a great ass!" This primary cross gender identification would seem to be rooted in the fact that he created the character himself from the available choices insuring a favorable, visual match and the realization that this form he had created, or chosen, was on display for others to see and, furthermore, operated as his primary line of contact with other players.

As potentially both an object of desire and subject of desire the game player comes to a rapid and sometimes uncomfortable identification with the avatar. My own experience with online games would seem to support this assertion as I have found that playing a female character invokes a deep-seated shyness that I normally repress. When playing *The Sims Online*, I created a character with my actual name and general physical characteristics. The combination was deadly for my enjoyment as the role-playing element was seriously reduced and my real life intruded into the rules of the virtual realm. The discomfort felt by my female friend was visited upon me as my doppelganger engaged in activities, primarily due to my inexperience with the game platform, for which I felt ashamed. The nature of the game was such that the adult content transgressed actions personably acceptable to me. However, my discomfort also belies the narrow gap between the pleasure in virtual role-playing and the player's self-image which is obfuscated to varying degrees by the science fiction or fantasy settings of other games where we may retreat from our in game actions with the rather thin excuse of "that is not really me." The same excuse one uses for any type of perceived transgression of personal or public persona. Role-playing is itself an expression of the persona and not simply scripted acting.

Baudrillard and Žižek would no doubt be drawn to *The Sims*, not so much for the pleasure of play but because more so than any other entertainment media, *The Sims* is a perfect representation of the intrusive potential of cyberspace.

The future of the body—homo-sapiens will be replaced with different breeds. Homo-solitus (originating from Sol system), Homo-opifex, Homo-nano, and Homo-atrox. All genetically engineered, chemically altered, and technologically enhanced. All engineered clones. Life will be a continuum of cloned and replicated selves enabling a never ending series of replicated bodies. The body at the time of "saving" (mapping the quantum state) is the self. Strangely enough, this replication of the body after death suggests that the player is the "Soul" who exists in higher reality "after death" but that the this is no heaven as the true pleasure/desire is to be in the game. In a way, this is not a fiction—the virtual body can be seen and experienced in not precisely felt or embodied.

And yet, sit long enough at the computer and the boundary between my body and the virtual body begins to erode. Like playing music or driving, there comes a point where the higher brain functions cease to consciously respond to the meat body and extend into the tools of the activity. In this case the tool is the computer and the player extends not only into the tool, but also the virtual environment enabled by that tool. The conscious experience of the payer extends into the collective imagination of cyberspace. The first person perspective adds to this extension. One runs the body like one runs a car—though the tires are not a contiguous part of the body, we feel them nonetheless and know when something is amiss.

This re-embodiment is not necessarily the common experience (or is it?), but it is a potential experience for the regular participant in the virtual realm. Even casual players can become unnerved by the barest experience of this re-embodiment into the simulacrum.

A friend of mine, a female professor of English in her late forties, who regularly emails and chats online about various topics which interest her (including an obsession with the Pittsburg Steelers), was deeply uncomfortable with both *Ultima Online* and *The Sims Online*. She rapidly became attracted to her characters after bare minutes of play. Both times she had nightmares about this "little me" running about in cyberspace without her. She found it a deeply unnerving experience and described her play as "dangerously addictive" and "very weird." She refuses to repeat the experience after the second attempt.

What did she find so disturbing? Her dream of a cyber-twin having its own existence without her, the creator, belies a primal source of the fear—like primitive cultures, she has expressed the fear that the image could steal the soul, the essence of the person.

Though this fear is unfounded in our culture (we do not believe that cameras or even computers can literally steal the soul, though we still do have fiction to that effect in both horror and science fiction, in particular cyberpunk), the fear nevertheless expresses the reality that a virtual existence is, in our culture, rapidly becoming a popular possibility. (Haraway's cyborg is already a virtual proposition. The joining of the body with the internet is the epitome of the virtual body.)

Foucault also posits subjectivity as virtual. Certainly sex has already moved into the realm of the virtual in Foucault's theory as it has moved out of act and into the discourse of the medico-juridical realm.

The body is always already virtual. We cannot locate it. The so-called natural body, that body which supposedly precedes language, culture, and power cannot be properly said to exist but rather as Lacan suggested is nothing more than an inarticulate desire to return to a time before individuation and the accompanying loss. We are virtual: and even more to the point we know we are even if we do not have the language to express the feeling as such. We are something other than our true selves. We do not feel like us. We do not feel or experience as we should. But in negating our virtuality in desiring a phantom of the lost self we negate who we are, what we have become, choosing rather the ephemeral nostalgia for a self that never was and never can be. Once born in this time, in this culture, indeed all of the so-called Western Cultures, any subjectivity other than the virtual becomes impossible. There can be no return for there is nowhere to return to. To move to Taiwan and become a Buddhist is simply to adopt one form of the virtual self in an attempt to exclude all others. There is no return from Virtuality. Standing in a hall of mirrors, overwhelmed by the multiple, layered images, we may choose one, focus on it to the exclusion of all others and say this one is me. But it is not for those other mirrors those other aspects of the virtual subject do not cease to be but rather continue to operate ignored beyond our consciousness. Ignored they do not die they threaten like so many Jungian shadows dancing in the darkness.

We find relief in cyberspace not because it is an escape from reality but because it is an admission of who and what we have become.

Social interaction is one of the main reasons MMOs exist. Like the traditional RPG, part of the attraction of MMOs is the ability to interact with others. Unlike MMOs, however, much of this interaction could be between people who have never met in real life—rather like the play by mail RPGs that were popular for a short while. There are always feats of heroism and daring. The very impermanence of death, until the virtual death of the entire world with the closing down of a gaming environment, authorizes and encourages boldness both of individuals and groups—though the would be hero at others expense, the player who forgets his place in the group will quickly find himself looking for new companions-alone online as s/he is at the computer. The virtual world can be cruel, in this it parallels what I grudgingly term "real life."

The notion of property as not only the *expression* of individuality, but the *creation* of it, is further expressed in games where characters may purchase (or build) housing. In *UO*, for example, a character can purchase buildings in a wide variety of styles (depending on availability) and decorate their hut or castle with an amazingly diverse selection of furniture, paintings, statues, and plants. As creative in housing decoration as in other elements of play, some players even assemble furnishings from non-decorative items to produce an endless variety. Players can build an "aquarium," for example, out of stacks of blue cloth and dead fish. The "recipes" for some of these items are available on the internet and some players even sell them, or their services (for virtual and real money), as "interior decorators," clearly a profession never anticipated by the designers. While houses help create the sense of character individuality and serve as the extension of the avatar, they do not create a complete illusion of RL: just as the avatar does not have a digestive system, the house does not have a toilet (though someone has no doubt figured out how to build one).

The fantasy landscape of *Ultima* is a jewel of a world: a vast detailed map with roads, rivers, mountains, desert islands, and tropical forests. But it is more than just a map for this map is an exact visual representation of exactly what it simulates-every tree stream and dell, every bird and flower, every person is represented in both form and action. I see myself, my avatar, move along the terrain. I see the bird I shoot with my bow and arrow, watch as its blood spills out on the ground as I cut it up to take the meat for cooking later and pluck the feathers destined for the shafts I will make from wood I will chop from that pine over there. As I chop the tree a woodsman passes. His name is Alphonse. I pause to wave and say Hello the tiny words appearing above my head on that map of everything becoming part of the landscape for a brief moment. Alphonse replies and I do not think of the person, the other player, sitting out there somewhere in the world, female or male. I see Alphonse and Alphonse sees me: sees Ximena-me.

Eleven: Virtual Lives

When philosopher of history and science Michel Serres wrote of "that rare and narrow passage" between the sciences of humanity and the exact sciences (18), he intended to suggest not only the infrequency and difficulty of such contact, but also the unwillingness on either side to engage in what could be a dangerous, low-profit venture. It seems a long haul back to our common origins in *philosophia*, and typically, efforts to regain common ground between the disciplines have approached the problem as a one-sided move from the exact sciences to the study of the humanities. Notable exceptions such as N. Katherine Hayles' *Chaos Bound: Orderly Disorder in Contemporary Literature and Science* do attempt to create the atmosphere of dialog; yet, while Hayles discusses how "Different disciplines are drawn to similar problems because the concerns underlying them are highly charged within a prevailing cultural context" (xi) her text still operates largely as a science-based approach to the study of cultural texts. Those in the humanities may agree to the applicability of complex dynamics and field theory to the study of culture, but the inverse is not typically true. For example, while we find Hayles' application of scientific theory to culture "interesting" or even "enlightening," works such as Donna J. Harraway's *Simians, Cyborgs and Women* are deemed "intrusive" and are largely ignored by the scientific community. Practical applications of scientific theories to specific works in the humanities may be useful, but in essence, these projects either simply advocate or court the sciences and rarely seek common parallels *in theory or practice* which are *mutually* supporting and enlightening. We need to look again at what we have always had in common, at something which prefigures even *philosophia*: the means of observation.

First, our bodies are the essential apparatus of all observation. We may think of "body" in these terms as the "mind-body complex," but the mind-body dichotomy is not necessary to the argument. Furthermore, based in our own sense of embodiment and observation of other bodies, our corporeality defines the starting

162

point and ultimate limit of human perception. In essence, as Carl Gustav Jung writes in **Archetypes and the Collective Unconscious,** "No one can escape from the prejudice of being human".[47] In the humanities, Jung's sentiment has become a virtual given of any postmodern critical approach to the study of culture and its artifacts. In the sciences, however, the role of the observer in the observation and collection of data is somewhat of a sore spot as many scientists are feeling the necessity to assert in strong terms the essentially "human nature" of observation which seems to undermine the notion of scientific objectivity.

Second, in scientific terms we are complex dynamical systems and this fact affects our observational capacity in a very real way. In the exact sciences, the critical problems of observation stem, at least in part, from the fields of quantum mechanics and of complex dynamical systems (more popularly Chaos Theory) where the objectivity of the human body as an observation "device"—via the eyes, nose, ears, mouth, brain, etc.—comes into question. As James Gleick writes in the often quoted *Chaos: Making of a New Science,*

> The paragon of a complex dynamical system and to many scientists, therefore, the touchstone of any approach to complexity is the human body. No object of study available to physicists offers such a cacophony of counter rhythmic motion on scales from macroscopic to microscopic: motion of muscles, of fluids of currents, of fibers of cells. No physical system has lent itself to such an obsessive brand of reductionism: every organ has its own micro-structure and its own chemistry, and student physiologists spend years just on the naming of the parts. Yet how ungraspable these parts can be![48]

The body, in these terms, is a complex dynamical system, and from this position of complex embodiment we speak, we observe, and we

---

[47] Carl Gustav Jung, *Archetypes and the Collective Unconscious*, 63.
[48] James Gleick, *Chaos: Making of a New Science*, 297.

produce knowledge. This fundamental fact ties all the disciplines together and supplies us with a common teleology, to maximize and improve observation.

It was the Enlightenment that consciously redefined the body as an apparatus of observation in order to observe, dominate, and eventually incorporate nature. In *The Dialectic of Enlightenment*, Max Horkheimer and Theodor W. Adorno argue that the scientific impetus of the Enlightenment was not a liberating move in the quest for truth, but a quest for a power which ultimately enslaves. They indicate the Enlightenment motto "knowledge, which is power, knows no obstacles"[49] as a type of confession of the true goals of the Enlightenment. The emphasis on the power of the individual is directly related to the drive to dominate nature, a drive that inevitably turns back on itself and leads to the formation of individuals who are internally repressed. As Foucault writes in *The Birth of the Clinic,* "What counts in the things said by men is not so much what they may have thought or the extent to which these things represent their thoughts, as that which systematizes them from the outset, thus making them thereafter endlessly accessible to new discourses and open to the task of transforming them".[50] All observation becomes standardized so that Sournia may write in *Logique et morale du diagnostic* that "We 'observe' [a patient] in the same way that we observe the stars or a laboratory experiment".[51] This relativization of the means of observation yields subjects whose function, in Horkeheimer and Adorno's terms, is to both add to the base of information as commodity or consume that commodity; subjects who are in Foucault's terms simultaneously reconstructed as both apparatus of observation (observer-bodies) and information production (subjects of the empirical gaze) where the whole relationship of signifier to signified is redistributed to the aims of observation. As he writes in *Discipline and Punish,*

---

[49] Horkheimer and Adorno, *The Dialectic of Enlightenment*, 4.
[50] Foucault, *The Birth of the Clinic*, xix.
[51] qtd. in Foucault, *The Birth of the Clinic*, xv.

The historical moment of the disciplines was the moment when an art of the human body was born, which was directed not only at the growth of its skills, nor at the intensification of its subjection, but at the formation of a relation that in the mechanism itself makes it more obedient as it becomes more useful, and conversely. . . . Discipline increases the forces of the body (in economic terms of utility) and diminishes these same forces (in political terms or obedience).[52]

Once subjects are redefined as apparatus of observation, observation itself necessarily reforms as a hierarchical structure as power is dissociated from the body and turned into an "aptitude" or "capacity." Discipline seeks to increase this capacity while at the same time changing the course of power so that while the subject becomes an ever more rigidly calibrated observation device the power associated with observation is bled away. In essence, the individual power associated with observation is reorganized towards the ends of observation in general.

This reconstruction of subjects as apparatus for observation yields more or less rigidly calibrated—educated and socialized—subjects who may be categorized as "objective" to varying degrees within the observational system. Even the shoddiest of human observers could still supply data for the interpretation even if they could not supply the "correct" interpretation themselves. Freud's Dora, for example, comments upon her own life and dreams, but it is only through the clarifying observation of Freud that we believe Dora or understand her in any meaningful way. This hierarchization of observation necessitates a chain of command which in turn implies an Ultimate Observer or Final Observation. In analytical psychology, for example, that Ultimate Observer is Freud himself as he designed and taught his theory and analyzed his "disciples" before sending them out to analyze others. Of all the possible meanings of Dora's dream of a burning house and "a jewel case,"

---

[52] Foclault, *Discipline and Punish*, 138.

Freud recontextualizes the information within his theory as "My 'jewel case' is in danger and if anything happens it will be father's fault." His higher-level observation effectively commits Dora's statement to a single context and a single reality where "jewel case" is symbolic of her vagina and the burning house the modus for her "loss" of it to Mr. K. The subject, then, can be imagined as caught in an infinite regress of observation all the way back to an inferred "Final Observer" who would be able to realize the fullness and meaning of the data. Of course, the fact that Dora ultimately rejected Freud's analysis reminds us that, at least on a local level, two realities can exist and hierarchical observation does not always have the intended effect on the observed.

The problems of interaction between observer and observed are fairly easy to understand when we are dealing with individual humans, especially when we consider that Freud's interpretations are no longer generally considered accurate. We simply do not all see the same way and generally accepted interpretations change over time, which is the very reason the scientific method was adopted in the first place in order to counteract individual subjectivity. As suggested earlier, the real problem of observation arises in the hard sciences and specifically in quantum mechanics where problems of subjectivity, supposedly eliminated (or greatly reduced) by the scientific method, re-emerge at the base of all observation in the smallest, most essential form of matter in the universe.

According to quantum mechanics, all reality is (to some degree) observer-dependent. "In general," Stephen Hawking writes in *A Brief History of Time: From the Big Bang to Black Holes*, "quantum mechanics does not predict a single definite result for an observation. Instead, it predicts a number of different possible outcomes and tells us how likely each of these is."[53] The difference in the possible outcomes is observer dependant and as John Gribbon explains in his *In Search of Schrödinger's Cat*, all vision involves

---

[53] Stephen Hawking, *A Brief History of Time: From the Big Bang to Black Holes*, 55.

bouncing protons of light off objects and into our eyes. A photon doesn't disturb large objects like a passing semi-truck on the Interstate very much, so we don't expect the tuck to be affected by simply looking at it, though we may wish it was. By looking at the truck, we *do* change it, though the change infinitesimally small. Observation effects everything we observe and ourselves. An electron, however, is so small that we have to use electromagnetic energy with a short wave-length in order to "see" it at all. And as Gribbon explains, "Such gamma radiation is very energetic, and any photon of gamma radiation that bounces off an electron and can be detected by our experimental apparatus will drastically change the position and momentum of the electron—of the electron is an atom, the very act of observing it . . . may knock it out of the atom altogether" effectively dismantling it.[54] At the particle level, the base for all other observation, observer and observed are intertwined and their paths forever changed by their interaction. Form this starting point in quantum mechanics emerged a theory which eventually had repercussions up the observational scale from the smallest particles to the universe.

To understand the full implication of what one particle could change we turn to Erwin Schrödinger's metaphorical cat. As he explains in "*Naturwiss*,"

> A cat is penned up in a steel chamber, along with the following diabolical device (which must be secured against direct interference by the cat): in a Geiger counter there is a tiny bit of radioactive substance, so small, that perhaps in the course of one hour one of the atoms decays, but also, with equal probability, perhaps none; if it happens, the counter tube discharges and through a relay releases a hammer which shatters a small flask of hydrocyanic acid. If one has left the entire system to itself for an hour, one would say the cat still lives *if* meanwhile no atom has decayed. The first atomic decay would have poisoned it.

---

[54] James Gleick, *Chaos: Making of a New Science*, 156-7.

The ψ[theta] function of the entire system would express this by having in it the living and the dead cat (pardon the expression) mixed or smeared out in equal parts.

The mathematical equation, for those interested, looks like the following where theta=1 over the square root of 2 (theta "dead" + theta "alive"):

$$\psi = \frac{1}{\sqrt{2}}(\psi_{dead} \times \psi_{alive}) + (\psi_{alive} \times \psi_{\text{human sees live cat}})$$

Schrödinger's metaphor is constructed as a cat in a sealed box with a vial of poison gas attached to a proton detector. If all circumstances are favorable to the creation of a proton, what happens to the cat? Is it alive or dead? According to quantum theory, the proton will at the same time be created and strike the detector and not be created and not strike the detector, so that the answer to Schrödinger's question is a paradoxical "yes and no." Without an outside observer opening the box and committing to one reality or another, then, theorists argued that both events have happened: live cat, dead cat. The implication is, as James Gleick summarizes, "Gone was the luxury of supposing that a single reality existed, that the human mind had reasonably clear access to it, and that the scientists could explain it."[55] Most physicists agree that there are five ways to resolve the paradox: the first is solipsism, or to assume that the only thing verifiable is the self so the seeming paradox is just part of everything else outside the self which cannot be known. Physicist would reject this possibility out of hand as inconsistent with the goals and means of science.

The second possibility, and generally considered the simplest, is that *any* being with consciousness can collapse the wave functions (the mathematical symbol of multiple cats) by

---

[55] James Gleick, *Chaos: Making of a New Science*, 14.

observation, effectively either committing the universe to one reality or another or identifying which universe we already occupy. Practically, the paradox is a local event contained in the box itself. This possibility is called the Copenhagen interpretation and as Barrow and Tippler summarize,

> According to quantum theory, it is necessary to include some physics of the observer or measuring apparatus in the analysis if one wishes to talk about the result of a measurement on a system. A moment's reflection will show that the essential feature of a measuring apparatus is the ability to record the result of a measurement. The essence of a successful measurement is the transfer of information about the system being measured to the memory of the apparatus . . . ."[56]

Which is to say, the act of observing properly and "recording" (or remembering) the data resolves the paradox. However, there is a further implication: "In the opinion of Heisenberg and Weizsäcker, the Copenhagen Interpretation implies that properties of objects do not exist until they are observed; the properties are 'latent' but are not 'actual' before the observation"[57] or that "the act of observation is responsible for bringing properties of physical systems into existence.[58] The third possibility is that a community of observers can collectively collapse wave-functions. One observer looks in the box which starts the process which is verified and solidified through the hierarchy of observation. Implicit in this interpretation is the effect of the observer on the system being observed. Fourth, there is some sort of Ultimate Observer who is responsible for the collapse of wave functions. In essence, the Final Observer is constructed as the un-observable, the last on the chain of observables who clarifies and solidifies all previous observation. The Judeo-Christian Jehovah

---

[56] John Barrow and Frank Tippler, *The Anthropic Cosmological Principle*, 472.
[57] Ibid. 468-9.
[58] Ibid. 463.

would fit the bill nicely as omniscience is the essence of the Final Observer and the fact of omniscience, in this case, actually explains omnipotence. In *The Physics of Immortality: Modern Cosmology, God and the Ressurection of the Dead* Tippler terms this Ultimate Observer the "Omega Point" (essentially our own descendants in the a galactic computer) which comes into being in the far future and from that position collapses all wave functions. Fifth, Wave functions never collapse (as there is no ultimate observer). The best known interpretation of this possibility is "Everett's Friends Paradox." With no Ultimate Observation, all possibilities are, mathematically at least, possible. As John Gribbon explains,

> Everett's interpretation [of Schrödinger's Cat] accepts the quantum equations entirely at face value and says that both cats are real. There is a live cat, and there is a dead cat; but they are located in different worlds. It is not that the radioactive atom inside the box either did or did not decay, but that it did both. Faced with this decision, the whole world—the universe—split into two versions of itself, identical in all respects except that in one version the atom decayed and the cat died, while in the other the atom did not decay and the cat lived.[59]

The opening of the box is not the moment when the universe splits but only the moment of recognition of to which universe the observer belongs. We might think of a series of observers going all the way back in history, but unlike the previous possibility, Everett suggests that as an observer is supplanted by another observer, he is observed and vice versa, therefore, for Everett's interpretation the Ultimate Observer is discounted as a mathematically logical possibility. The Ultimate Observer is simply a paradoxical answer to a paradox because an observer cannot exist who is not observed (or, if she was observed she would not be the Ultimate Observer at all, and so on.)

---

[59] John Gribbon, *In Search of Schrödinger's Cat: Quantum Physics and Reality*, 238.

The interpretations of Schrödinger's Cat applied not only to quantum mechanics, but to many of the other sciences as well, because as Tippler writes, "everything in sight is a quantum system," and that includes us humans as well.[60]

Based on our role as quantum-system observers, Barrow and Tippler, among others, developed what has come to be called The Anthropic Cosmological Principle: a series of principles focused on the role of the observer in the Universe based on quantum mechanics and defined under one rubric.

The basic fact of observation derived from Quantum Mechanics, according to Barrow and Tippler, is that "we are a carbon-based life-form which spontaneously evolved on an earth-like planet around a star of G-2 spectral type, and any observation we make is necessarily self-selected by this absolutely fundamental fact." Our bodies, in essence, are measuring devices "whose self-selection properties *must* be taken into account, just as astronomers *must* take into account the self-selection properties of optical telescopes."[61] This selection effect suggests that data is limited by what can be observed; i.e. the smallest "quanta" is now a quark because we can't see anything smaller (yet). All of which implies that that we must always take into accounts the limits of the observation devices we use beginning with the device which is "us." In other words, what we have come to call "the subject" is an observation apparatus fine-tuned to observe the universe from the smallest quanta, to the mundane motes of dust, to the galactic rim. But, to what end? Well, as Robert Penn Warren's Jack Burden states in *All the King's Men*, "The end of man is to know." Complete observation is both our *telos* (purpose) and *thanatos* (end).

The base premise of the Anthropic Cosmological Principle states that we cannot conceive of a universe without us because we would not be in that universe to conceive of it. The very term "without us" asserts that we are here, and any conception can only

---

[60] Frank J. Tippler, *The Physics of Immortality: Modern Cosmology, God and the Ressurection of the Dead* , 31.

[61] John Barrow and Frank J. Tippler, *The Anthropic Cosmological Principle*, 3.

be in comparison to our presence; the *a priori* of observation is the presence of an observer. As Barrow and Tippler explain, "The Anthropic Principles seek to link aspects of the global and local structure of the Universe to these conditions necessary for the existence of living observers."[62] In essence,

> [T]he basic features of the Universe, including such properties as its shape, size, age and laws must be *observed* to be of a type that allows the evolution of observers, for if intelligent life did not evolve in an otherwise possible universe, it is obvious that no one would be asking the reason for the observed shape, size, age and so forth of the universe.[63]

The Anthropic Cosmological Principle is broken down by Barrow and Tippler into three separate postulates: "The Weak Anthropic Principle" (or WAP), "The Strong Anthropic Principle" (SAP), and "The Final Anthropic Principle" (FAP).

The Weak Anthropic Principle states that "The observed values of all physical and cosmological quantities are not equally probable but they take on values restricted by the requirement that there exist sites where carbon-based life can evolve, and by the requirement that the Universe be old enough for it to have already done so."[64] Or, to restate, only on a planet where carbon-based life and intelligence evolves is it possible to wonder about the origin of carbon-based life in the Universe. Barrow and Tippler make the distinction of "carbon-based" life because other universes could conceivably evolve without "us" (carbon-based intelligence) with non-carbon-based intelligence, but these universes would not necessarily include us. In this view, intelligence is not a necessary, but a sufficient condition for the presence or creation of the Universe.

---

[62] John Barrow and Frank Tippler. *The Anthropic Cosmological Principle*, 3.
[63] Ibid. 1-2.
[64] Ibid. 16.

The Strong Anthropic Principle posits that "The Universe must have those properties which allow life to develop within it at some stage in its history."[65] This view supports several other possibilities. First, there exists one possible Universe "designed" with the goal of generating and sustaining observers, which suggests that the *a priori* of the Universe is *mind*. We could say that intelligence, wherever it might exist, is equivalent on the galactic scale to the frontal lobe in man and the other higher mammals. Even more, the sum total of all minds in the Universe *is* the frontal lobe of the Universe, or will be at some point in the future.

Second, the SAP suggests that observers are necessary to bring the Universe into being (this premise is also called the Participatory Anthropic Principle, or PAP), which is basically an extension of the previous proposition with the exception that the Universe does not exist as such until it "knows itself" through the evolution of intelligence. There are some interesting lines of influence between this view and Marx's First Historical moment and we could say, in essence, that the Universe does not enter history until it evolves intelligence to interact with it through the work of observation. Finally, the SAP suggests that an ensemble of other, different universes are necessary for the existence of our Universe.[66] Which is to say that "all possible worlds" must exist in order for this universe to exist.

The Final Anthropic Principle (FAP) is stated as "Intelligent information-processing must come into existence in the Universe, and, once it comes into existence, it will never die out."[67] The FAP suggests that "information processing" is central to the existence of the Universe, or as Timothy Leary jokes in his popular work on complex dynamics, *Chaos and Cyberculture*, the "you-niverse." In this case, the evolution of intelligence is a necessary condition to the existence of the Universe, and is, in a word the *reason* the Universe comes into existence at all.

---

[65] Barrow and Frank Tippler. *The Anthropic Cosmological Principle,* 21.
[66] Ibid. 22.
[67] Ibid. 23.

The Anthropic Principle, in each of its various forms, is a cosmic extension of Heisenberg's Uncertainty Principle and the theories behind Schrödinger's Cat Paradox, extensions which attempt "to restrict the structure of the Universe by asserting that intelligent life, or at least life in some form, in some way selects out the actual Universe from among the different imaginable universes: the only 'real' universes are those which can contain intelligent life, or at the very least contain some form of life."[68] In sum, intelligent life exists in the Universe and must exist in order to "know" the Universe, or any part of it, at all which may be one of many possible universes, and/or by that observation to "realize" the Universe, which may be the only Universe or one of many, any one of which might be dependent upon observers. As long as intelligent information processing exists the Universe will exist, and is, in effect its *raison d' être*.

The Universe and intelligence (of which humans are at least a part) are inter-dependent in a complex system of interaction that is evolving from intelligence towards complete, complex observation. In the Anthropic Cosmological Principles, observation is the first tool which humans use to remake their universe, and by extension and feed-back, internalize the Universe. The rest of the discussion will support, to some extent, the Weak and Strong Anthropic Principles, but it is in the Final Anthropic Principle that we find the most use for critical positioning to the effect that the Universe cannot exist without the observer. And it is from the position that intelligence exists in order to observe that we return to Foucault and the Panopticon.

In *Discipline and Punish*, Michel Foucault critiques Jeremy Bentham's now infamous Panopticon vision of the prison which is constructed with a central tower and surrounding cells. "In short," Foucault writes, "it reduces the principle of the dungeon; or rather of its three functions--to enclose, to deprive of light and to hide—it preserves only the first and eliminates the other two. Full lighting

---

[68] Frank J. Tippler *The Physics of Immortality: Modern Cosmology, God and the Ressurection of the Dead*, 511.

and the eye of a supervisor capture better than darkness . . . .
Visibility is a trap."[69] The ultimate goal of the Panopticon is "to
induce in the inmate a state of consciousness and permanent
visibility that assures the automatic functioning of power . . . .
[P]ower should be visible and unverifiable."[70] In essence, "The
Panopticon is a machine for dissociating the see/being seen dyad: in
the peripheric ring, one is totally seen, without ever seeing; in the
central tower, one sees everything without being seen."[71]

Foucault's point, of course, is not just that the Panopticon existed
in Bentham's vision and in practical application in prisons, but that
the power structure it represents exists everywhere in our culture.
We must remember that this spreading of the Panopticon was
Bentham's ultimate goal; furthermore the prison is but a poor
shadow of what he intended as the prison plan does not allow the
prisoners to observe the observers nor the observers to also be
observed. In society at large, however, the Panopticon operates so
that an observer may observe at a single glance, not only the
subjects of observation, but also other observers as well, and the
observer must always assume that s/he is also observed.[72] The
Panopticon is the product of a long process of the internalization of
observation within the subject with its progression from public
tortures and executions to the physical movement of punishments
from public to internal spaces. Foucault is clear that the process of
internalization of observation is an ongoing one. On this point,
Tippler and Foucault are in complete agreement as both would say
that observation has become central and is increasing. Foucault
would characterize this increase in observation as serving the needs
of power while Tippler would say the increase in observation is
teleological and leads to the Omega Point and the survival of
intelligence in the Universe. However, this is simply a matter of
scale as on the human level observation reinforces power which
leads to yet more observation *ad infinitum*, the logical outcome of

[69] Michel Foucault, *Discipline and Punish: The Birth of the Prison*, 200.
[70] Ibid. 201.
[71] Ibid. 202.
[72] Ibid. 207.

which would be progressive expansion until the entire universe was continually under reciprocal observation at every point at all times. This outcome is not only analogous to the Omega Point, *it is* the Omega Point. But, is this what Foucault intended when he wrote *Discipline and Punish*?

Most critics read Foucault's critical retelling of the history of the prison as proscriptive rather than descriptive, or at the very least use his theory as such. This *use* of philosophy and history is as old as philosophy itself and gave rise to, for example, Neo-classicism with the reinterpretation of Aristotle's unities of Time, Place, and Action as prescriptive of the perfect drama for all places and times. Oedipus Rex may have been the perfect play for Aristotle, but that is not to say that it is the perfect play for all times nor that Aristotle intended his description of his "perfect" play to be prescriptive for all future dramatists. Aristotle himself was certainly not averse to brilliant innovation. This reaction to panopticism, however, is quite understandable as panopticism, at least in Occidental culture, is a continual source of fear and paranoia. We might think here of projective works such as George Orwell's *1984* which predict one ultimate outcome of such as process. Even more contemporary, popular works like *Star Trek: The Next Generation* and *Voyager* express the fear of panopticism as a major, recurring theme in the ever-popular Borg episodes.[73]

This fear of panopticism has roots in Occidental mythology and finds its major expression in the Tower of Babel myth where the greatest sin was, according to the word of Jehovah, that the people should unite: "And the Lord said, Behold, the people *is* one, and they have all one language; and this they begin to do: and now nothing will be restrained from them, which they have imagined to do."[74] As Michel Serres interprets, "An ingenious, intelligent, organized, articulate, and sedulous people undertake to build. The

---

[73] The Borg, described variously as a "collective" and a "hive," is an alien species which incorporates minds, bodies, and technology into itself. In the Borg society, no thoughts or actions are private and there is no individuality as all actions are unilaterally "seen" by all members of the collective.

[74] Genesis 11.6, King James Version.

Tower of Babel will reach the sky. Near the end, however, the project fails, so it is said, through a confusion of tongues. In the desert there will remain some stones, a whole gigantic ruin slowly split and slaked by waters and wind, mastic trees, frost."[75] They would have been the people who, with the panoptical technology of the tower, could see unilaterally and universally. They would have been able to see the pattern of life passing below them, see their borders, any of them and all of them. The fulfillment of the Panopticon is what Jehovah tried to stop because Jehovah is already at the center of the Panopticon. Panopticism, true panopticism, undermines and displaces Jehovah (the "high tower" of Psalms) as all intelligence would be able to "see" unilaterally.

Donna J. Harraway's voicing of the "new myth" of the cyborg, in *Simians, Cyborgs, and Women*, is an important step in the direction of unilateral vision which begins in panopticism. As she writes, "Vision in this technological feast becomes unregulated gluttony; all perspective gives way to infinitely mobile vision, which no longer seems just mythically about the god-trick of seeing everything from nowhere, but to have put the myth into ordinary practice. And like the god-trick, this eye fucks the world to make techno-monsters. . . . But of course that view of infinite vision is an illusion, a god-trick."[76] And more:

> We need to learn our bodies, endowed with primate color and stereoscopic vision, how to attach the objective to our theoretical and political scanners in order to name where we are and are not, in dimensions of mental and physical space we hardly know how to name. So, not so perversely, objectivity turns out to be about particular and specific embodiment, and definitely not about the false vision promising transcendence of all limits and responsibility.

[75] Michel Serres, *Genesis* (Trans. Geneviève James and James Nielson. Anne Arbor: U of Michigan P, 1995) 123.

[76] Donna J. Haraway, *Simians, Cyborgs and Women: The Reinvention of Nature* (New York: Routledge, 1991) 189.

> The moral is simple: only partial perspective promises objective vision.[77]

Objectivity, then, has nothing to do with grand scale observation, as suggested by quantum mechanics and the Anthropic Cosmological Principle. The Panopticon, originally conceived in the tower and its extension, the observatory, is effectively an observatory internalized. C. G. Jung addresses just such an issue when he writes of Archetypes that "Endless repetition has engraved these experiences into our psychic constitution, not in the form of images filled with content, but at first only as *forms without content*, representing merely the possibility of a certain type of perception and action".[78] Foucault's rendering of the Panopticon is a contemporary archetypal representation which is internalized so that the subject carries with them an ever-present observation as the *a priori* of action. But, need this be a source of fear? There is no evidence that Foucault intended to suggest anything other than the realization of the fact of observation as a critical necessity. In fact, we could say that if Foucault was advocating anything at all it would be self-awareness of the role of observation in the function of power. He is perfectly clear that observation is inescapable and the best we can hope for is slight modifications in the cycles of inscribing observation. If, as the Anthropic Cosmological Principle asserts, the purpose of intelligence is observation, then the *telos*, or end, of intelligence is optimum observation where intelligence serves the needs of observation and not inverse.

By my reading Foucault's critical interpretation of the Panopticon and the Anthropic Cosmological principle are not only analogous, but mutually supporting. Foucault has hypothesized at the societal level what is already established (in theory) in physics at the quantum level and in Cosmology at the cosmic level. The three parts of the puzzle fit nicely together and it is a very short reach

[77] Donna J. Haraway, *Simians, Cyborgs and Women: The Reinvention of Nature* (New York: Routledge, 1991) 190.
[78] Carl Gustav Jung, *The Archetypes and the Collective Unconscious* (Trans. C. F. Hull. Bollingen Series XX, Princeton, NJ: Princeton UP, 1990) 48.

indeed to convert Foucault into physics and vice-versa. In both the Panopticon and the Anthropic Principles, the human is a transient phase observation apparatus which will be outmoded (probably in the far future) in the interests of the evolution of observation. If observation is the purpose of intelligence in the Universe, then anything which stands in the way of complete (unilateral and non-hierarchical) observation is questionable at best. Our end, our *telos* and transformation through death of the human subject, is to eliminate obstacles to observation. The Anthropic Principles already have a term for this unity of observation: the Omega Point.

Finally, it is my contention that the Enlightenment redefined the body as an apparatus of critical observation stationed within an observational hierarchy which presumes a "final" observation or "theory of everything." Traditional science, however, rejects teleology as a prejudice of the observer in an attempt to "objectify" observation. This rejection of teleological hypotheses is one of the fundamental divisions between the hard sciences and sciences of humanity as, by their very nature the sciences of humanity operate on teleological premises. The various forms of the Anthropic Cosmological Principle, however, rooted in quantum mechanics and complex dynamics consciously incorporate this teleological view inherent in the dynamics of observation and thereby reconnect themselves with the sciences of humanity at the observational cornerstone of thought. The path of observation is the most fundamental and accessible route in the project of a mutually supporting theory between the disciplines. Primary to the goal of observation is the exploration of borders, boundaries and so-called "givens," and most importantly, anything constructed as "natural." This project is already underway, but needs a new impetus. The conflation of the panoptical theory of power with the Anthropic Cosmological Principle will serve as the theoretical bridge between the sciences of humanity and the exact sciences. The technology of observation must be *self-consciously* incorporated and expanded. The observed must become the observer and vice-versa *ad infinitum* until hierarchy as such comes to mean as little as "0" without "1."

Twelve: Bibliography

Alinovi, Francesco. *Resident Evil: Spopravvivere all'orrore*. Milan, Italy: Edizioni Unicopli, 2003.

Anderson, Peter B., Berit Holmqvist and Jen F. Jensen. *The Computer as Medium*. Cambridge, MA: Cambridge UP, 1992.

Bakhtin, Mikhail. *Rabelais and His World*. Trans. Helene Iswolsky. Bloomington: Indiana UP, 1984.

Balsamo, Anne. *Technologies of the Gendered Body: Reading Cyborg Women*. Durham, NC: Duke UP, 1996.

Barr, Marleen, ed. *Future Females, The Next Generation: New Voices and Velocities in Feminist Science Fiction Criticism*. Boulder, CO: Rowman & Littlefield, 2000.

Barrow, John, and Frank Tippler. *The Anthropic Cosmological Principle*. New York: Oxford UP, 1986.

Bartokowski, Frances. *Feminist Utopias*. Lincoln: U of Nebraska P, 1989.

Bates, Bob. *Game Design: The Art and the Business of Creating Games*. Roseville, CA: Premier, 2002.

Baudrillard, Jean. *Simulations*. Trans. Paul Foss, Paul Patton and Philip Beitchman. New York: Simiotext[e], 1983.

Beauvoir, Simone de. *The Second Sex*. Trans. and ed. H.M. Parshley. New York: Vintage, 1989.

Bell-Metereau, Rebecca. *Hollywood Androgyny*. New York: Columbia University Press, 1985.

Bloomer, Jennifer. "Big Jugs." *The Hysterical Male*. Ed. Arthur and Marilouise Kroker. New York: St. Martin's, 1991.

Booker, M. Keith. *Techniques of Subversion in Modern Literature*. Gainesville: UP of Florida, 1991.

Brandt, Peter. "Somewhere in the Forest." *Twentieth Century Literature* 42.1 (1996): 88-102.

Broderick, Mick. "Heroic Apocalypse: Mad Max, Mythology and the Millennium." In *Crisis Cinema: the Apocalyptic Idea in Postmodern Narrative*. Ed. Christopher Sharrett. Washington, DC: Maisonneuve, 1993. 251-72.

Broege, Valerie. "Electric Eve: Images of Female Computers in Science Fiction." In *Clockwork Worlds: Mechanized Environments in SF*. Ed. Richard D. Erlich and Thomas P. Dunn. Westport, CT: 1983. 183-94.

Brooke-Rose, Christine. A Rhetoric of the Unreal: Studies in Narrative and Structure, Especially of the Fantastic. Cambridge: Cambridge UP, 1992.

Brosnan, John. The Primal Screen. London: Hazell, 1991.

Brownmiller, Susan. Against Our Will: Men, Women, and Rape. New York: Fawcett Columbine, 1993.

Brunner, Cornelia, Dorothy Bennet, and Margaret Honey, "Girl Games and Technological Desire," *Barbie to Mortal Kombat: Gender and Computer Games*. Ed. Justine Cassell and Henry Jenkins. Cambridge, MA: MIT Press, 1999.

Bukatman, Scott. *Terminal Identity: The Virtual Subject in Postmodern Science Fiction*. Durham, NC: Duke UP, 1993.

Butler, Judith. *Antigone's Claim: Kinship Between Life and Death*. New York: Columbia UP, 2000.

Butler, Judith. *Bodies that Matter: On the Discursive Limits of "Sex."* New York: Routledge, 1993.

Butler, Judith. *Gender Trouble: Feminism and the Subversion of Identity*. New York: Routledge, 1990.

Calamosca, Fabio. *Final Fantasy: Vivere tra gli indigeni del cyberspace*. Milan, Italy: Edizioni Unicopli, 2003.

Campbell, Joseph. *The Hero with a Thousand Faces*. Bollingen Series XVII. Princeton, NJ: Princeton UP, 1973.

Campbell, Joseph. *The Masks of God: Oriental Mythology*. New York, Penguin, 1991.

Campbell, Joseph. *The Masks of God: Primitive Mythology*. New York: Penguin, 1991.

Campbell, Joseph. *The Power of Myth*. New York: Doubleday, 1988.

Carroll, Lewis. *Alice's Adventures in Wonderland. The Complete Illustrated Works of Lewis Carroll*. Ed. Edward Guiliano. New York: Avenel, 1982. 1-80.

Carroll, Lewis. *Sylvie and Bruno. The Complete Illustrated Works of Lewis Carroll*. Ed. Edward Guiliano. New York: Avenel, 1982. 491-654.

Carroll, Lewis. *Through the Looking Glass. The Complete Illustrated Works of Lewis Carroll*. Ed. Edward Guiliano. New York: Avenel, 1982. 81-75.

Cartwright, Frederick F. and Michael D. Biddiss. *Disease and History*. New York: Barnes and Noble, 1991.

Certeau, Michel de. *Heterologies: Discourse on the Other*. Trans. Brian Massumi. *Theory and History of Literature*. Vol. 17. Minneapolis: U of Minnesota P, 1986.

Chodorow, Nancy. *The Reproduction of Mothering*. Berkeley: U of California P, 1978.

Chunovic, Louis. *One Foot on the Floor: The Curious Evolution of Sex on Television from* I Love Lucy *to* South Park. New York: TV Books, 2000.

Cirlot, J. E. *A Dictionary of Symbols*. 2nd ed. Trans. Jack Sage. New York: Philosophical Library, 1971.

Clover, Carol J. *Men, Women, and Chainsaws: Gender in the Modern Horror Film*. Princeton: Princeton UP, 1992.

Cohen, Jeffrey J., ed. *Monster Theory: Reading Culture*. Minneapolis: U of Minnesota P, 1996.

Connerton, Paul. *How Societies Remember*. Cambridge: Cambridge UP, 1989.

Creed, Barbara. "Gynesis, Postmodernism and the Science Fiction Horror Film." In *Alien Zone: Cultural Theory and Contemporary Science Fiction Cinema*. Ed. Annette Kuhn. New York: Verso, 1990. 128-44.

Creed, Barbara. "Lesbian Bodies: Tribades, Tomboys and Tarts." In *Sexy Bodies: The Strange Carnalities of Feminism*. Eds. E. Grosz and E Probyn. London: Routledge, 1995.

Creed, Barbara. *The Monstrous Feminine: Film, Feminism, Psychoanalysis*. New York: Routledge, 1997.

Davies, Jude and Carol R. Smith. *Gender, Ethnicity and Sexuality in Contemporary American Film*. Edinburgh: Keele UP, 1997.

Davies, Philip John and Paul Wells, eds. *American Film and Politics from Reagan to Bush Jr.* New York: Manchester UP, 2002.

Duchet-Suchaux, G. and M. Pastoreau. *The Bible and the Saints.* New York: Flammarion, 1994.

Ellison, Ralph. *Shadow and Act.* New York: Random, 1964.

Ermarth, Elizabeth Deeds. *Sequel to History: Postmodernism and the Crisis of Representational Time.* Princeton, NJ: Princeton UP, 1991.

Fernbach, Amanda. *Fantasies of Fetishism: from Decadence to the Posthuman.* New Brunswick, NJ: Rutgers UP, 2002.

Feynmen, Richard P. "Theory of Positrons." *Physical Review* 76 (1949): 749-59.

Fiedler, Leslie. *Freaks: Myths and Images of the Secret Self.* New York: Touchstone, 1978.

Fischer, Lucy. *Cinematernity: Film, Motherhood, Genre.* Princeton, NJ: Princeton UP, 1996.

Foster, Gwendolyn A. *Captive Bodies: Postcolonial Subjectivity in Cinema.* Albany: SUNY Press, 1999.

Foucault, Michel. *Discipline and Punish: The Birth of the Prison.* Trans. Alan Sheridan. New York: Vintage, 1995.

Foucault, Michel. *The Birth of the Clinic: An Archeology of Medical Perception.* Trans. A. M. Sheridan Smith. New York: Vintage, 1994.

Foucault, Michel. *The History of Sexuality: Volume I: An Introduction.* Trans. Robert Hurley. New York: Vintage, 1996.

Foucault, Michel. *This Is Not a Pipe.* Trans. James Harkness. Berkeley: U of California P, 1983.

Fowles, John. *The French Lieutenant's Woman.* 1969. New York: Signet, 1981.

Freud, Sigmund. *The Standard Edition of the Complete Psychological Works of Sigmund Freud.* 24 vols. Ed. James Strachey. New York, Norton, 2000.

Gardner, Martin, ed. *The Annotated Alice.* By Lewis Carroll. New York: Penguin, 1987.

Gardner, Martin. *The Ambidextrous Universe*. 1964. New York: Basic, 1967.

Gee, James Paul. *What Videogames Have to Teach Us About Learning and Literacy*. New York: Palgrave, 2003.

Gibson, William. *All Tomorrow's Parties*. New York: Berkley, 2003.

Gibson, William. *Idoru*. New York: Berkley, 1997.

Gibson, William. *Neuromancer*. New York: Ace, 2004.

Gleick, James. *Chaos: Making of a New Science*. New York: Penguin, 1987.

Gleick, James. *Genius: The Life and Science of Richard Feynman*. New York: Pantheon, 1992.

Goldberge, Lee et. al. *Science Fiction Filmaking in the 1980s*. Jefferson: McFarland, 1995.

Gould, George M. and Walter L. Pyle. *Anomalies and Curiosities of Medicine*. Electronic Text Center, University of Virginia Library.

Graham, Elaine L. *Representations of the Post/Human: Monsters, Aliens and Others in Popular Culture*. New Brunswick, NJ: Rutgers UP, 2002.

Grant, Barry Keith. *The Dread of Difference: Gender and the Horror Film*. Austin, TX: U of Texas P, 1996.

Gribbon, John. *In Search of Schrödinger's Cat: Quantum Physics and Reality*. New York: Bantum, 1984.

Gribbon, John. *Schrödinger's Kittens and the Search for Reality*. New York: Little, 1995.

Grossberg, Lawrence, Cary Nelson and Paula Treichler, eds. *Cultural Studies*. New York: Routledge, 1992.

Grosz, Elizabeth. "Freaks." *Social Semiotics* 1, no. 2 (1991): 25.

Harari, Josué V., and David F. Bell. "Introduction: Journal à plusieurs voies." *Hermes: Literature, Science, Philosophy*. By Michel Serres. Ed. Josué V. Harari and David F. Bell. Baltimore: Johns Hopkins UP, 1982. ix-xl.

Haraway, Donna J. *Simians, Cyborgs and Women: The Reinvention of Nature*. New York: Routledge, 1991.

Hartouni, Valerie. "Containing Women: Reproductive Discourse in the 1980s." In *Technoculture*. Ed. Constance Penley and Andrew Ross. Minneapolis: U of Minnesota P, 1991. 27-56.

Haskell, Molly. *Holding My Own in No Man's Land: Women and Men and Film and Feminists*. New York: Oxford UP, 1997.

Haskell, Molly. *From Reverence to Rape: The Treatment of Women in the Movies*. New York: Holt, Rinehart, and Winston, 1974.

Hawking, Stephen. *A Brief History of Time: From the Big Bang to Black Holes*. New York: Bantam, 1988.

Hayles, N. Katherine. *Chaos Bound: Orderly Disorder in Contemporary Literature and Science*. Ithaka: Cornell UP, 1990.

Hayles, N. Katherine. *How We Became Posthuman: Virtual Bodies in Cybernetics, Literature, and Informatics*. Chicago: U of Chicago P, 1999.

Helford, Elyce Rae. "Postfeminism and the Female Action-Adventure Hero: Positioning *Tank Girl*." In *Future Females, The Next Generation: New Voices and Velocities in Feminist Science Fiction Criticism*. Ed. Marleen S. Barr. Lanham, MA: Rowman & Littlefield, 2000. 291-308.

Hess, Elizabeth. *Yib's Guide to MOOing.* Trafford, 2006.

Holland, Walter, Henry Jenkins, and Kurt Squire. In *The Video Game Theory Reader*. Ed. Mark J. P. Wolf and Bernard Perron. New York: Routledge, 2003. 25-46.

Hollinger, Veronica and Joan Gordon, eds. *Edging Into the Future: Science Fiction and Contemporary Cultural Transformation*. Philadelphia: University of Pennsylvania Press, 2002.

Hong, Sung Joo. "A Study of Multiple Ending [sic] in The French Lieutenant's Woman: A Trace of Fowles' Disconcerting Voice." *The Journal of English Language as Literature* 38.3 (1992): 571-84.

Horkheimer, Max and Theodor W. Adorno. *The Dialectic of Enlightenment*. Trans. John Cumming. New York: 1982.

Horsley, Jake. *The Blood Poets: A Cinema of Savagery 1958-1999*. 2 vols. Lanham, MD: Scarecrow, 1999.

Hutcheon, Linda. *Narcissistic Narrative: The Metafictional Paradox*. Waterloo: Wilfred Laurier UP, 1980.

Jameson, Frederic. *Postmodernism or, the Cultural Logic of Late Capitalism*. Durham: Duke UP, 2001.

Jancovich, Mark. *Horror*. London: B.T. Batsford, 1992.

Jeffords, Susan. *Hard Bodies: Hollywood Masculinity in the Reagan Era*. New Brunswick: Rutgers UP, 1994.

Jenkins, Henry. "Combat Zone: Game Grrlz Talk Back," *From Barbie to Mortal Kombat*: *Gender and Computer Games*, Ed. Justine Cassell and Henry Jenkins. Cambridge, MA: MIT Press, 1999.

Jones, Steven G. *Virtual Culture. Identity and Communication in Cybersociety*. London: Sage Publications Ltd., 1997.

Jung, Carl Gustav. *The Archetypes and the Collective Unconscious*. Trans. C. F. Hull. Bollingen Series XX. Princeton, NJ: Princeton UP, 1990.

King, Lucien, ed. *Game On: The History and Culture of Videogames*. New York: Universe Publishing, 2002.

Klock, Geoff. *How to Read Superhero Comics and Why*. New York: Continuum, 2002.

Kristeva, Julia. *Powers of Horror: An Essay on Abjection*. Trans. Leon S. Roudiez. New York: Columbia UP, 1982.

Kroker, Arthur and Marilouise, eds. *Body Invaders: Panic Sex in America*. CultureTexts Series. Montreal: New World Perspectives, 1987.

Kroker, Arthur and Marilouise, eds. *The Hysterical Male: New Feminist Theory*. New York: St. Martin's, 1991.

Kuhn, Annette, ed. *Alien Zone II: The Spaces of Science Fiction Cinema*. New York: Verso, 1999.

Kuhn, Annette, ed. *Alien Zone: Cultural Theory and Contemporary Science Fiction Cinema*. New York: Verso, 1990.

Kuhn, Annette. *Women's Pictures: Feminism and Cinema*. New York: Verso, 1993.

Laqueur, Thomas. *Making Sex: Body and Gender from the Greeks to Freud*. Cambridge, MA: Harvard University Press, 1990.

Leary, Timothy. *Chaos and Cyberculture*. Ed. Michael Horowitz. Berkeley: Ronin, 1994.

Leonard, Linda Schierse. *Meeting the Madwoman: An Inner Challenge for Feminine Spirit*. New York: Bantam: 1993.

Lewis, Lisa A. *Gender Politics and MTV: Voicing the Difference*. Philadelphia: Temple UP, 1990.

Lewis-Williams, David. *The Mind in the Cave: Consciousness and the Origins of Art*. London: Thames & Hudson, 2004.

Loftus, Elizabeth F. and Geoffrey R. *Mind at Play: The Psychology of Videogames*. New York: Basic Books, 1983.

Luban, Pascal. *Designing and Integrating Puzzles in Action Adventure Games*. 14 July 2004. Available: www.gamasutra.com. 2002.

Luban, Pascal. *Turning a Linear Story into a Game: the Missing Link between Fiction and Interactive Entertainment.* 14 July 2004. Available: www.gamasutra.com. 2001.

Lundsgaard, Lene and Nina Norgaard comp. and annot. "New Orientations in Women's Literature." In *The Female Hero: An Anthology of Literary Texts on Women's Quests*. Copenhagen: Scriptor, 1985.

Lunenfel, Peter. *The Digital Dialectic: New Essays on New Media*. Cambridge, MA: The MIT Press, 1999.

Macdonald, Myra. *Representing Women: Myths of Femininity in the Popular Media*. New York: Edward Arnold, 1995.

Marks, Elaine and Isabelle de Courtivron, eds. *New French Feminisms: An Anthology*. New York: Schoken, 1981.

Mayne, Judith. *Cinema and Spectatorship*. New York: Routledge, 1993.

McMahon, Alison. "Immersion, Engagement, and Presence: A method for Analyzing 3-D Video Games." In *The Video Game Theory Reader*. Ed. Mark J. P. Wolf and Bernard Perron. New York: Routledge, 2003. 67-86.

Menville, Douglas, and R. Reginald with Mary A. Burgess. *Futurevisions: The New Golden Age of the Science Fiction Film*. San Bernadino, CA: The Borgo Press, 1985.

Mitchell, William J. *City of Bits: Space, Place, and the Infobahn.* Cambridge: MIT Press, 1995.

Mitchell, William J. *eTopia:"Urban Life, Jim—But not as we Know it."* Cambridge: MIT Press, 2000.

Mitchell, William J. *ME++: The Cyborg Self and the Networked City.* Cambridge: MIT Press, 2003.

Modeleski, Tania. *Feminism Without Women: Culture and Criticism in a "Postfeminist" Age.* New York: Routledge, 1991.

Mulvey, Laura. *Visual and Other Pleasures.* Bloomington: Indiana UP, 1989.

Murphy, Cullen. *The Word According to Eve.* New York: Mariner, 1999.

Murray, Janet H. *Hamlet on the Holodeck: The Future of Narrative in Cyberspace.* New York: The Free Press, 1997.

Myers, Richard. *S-F2: A Pictorial History of Science Fiction Films From "Rollerball" to "Return of the Jedi."* Secaucus, NJ: Citadel Press, 1984.

Pagels, Elaine. *Adam, Eve, and the Serpent.* New York: Vintage, 1988.

Paglia, Camille. *Sexual Personae: Art and Decadence from Nefertiti to Emily Dickinson.* New York: Vintage, 1991.

Penley, Constance, ed. *Feminism and Film Theory.* New York: Routledge: 1988.

Penley, Constance, Elisabeth Lyon, Lynn Spigel, and Janet Bergstrom, eds. *Close Encounters: Film, Feminism and Science Fiction.* Minneapolis: U of Minnesota P, 1991.

Penley, Constance. "Time Travel, Primal Scene and Critical Dystopia." In *Alien Zone: Cultural Theory and Contemporary Science Fiction Cinema.* Ed. Annette Kuhn. New York:Verso, 1990. 116-27. Reprinted in *Close Encounters: Film, Feminism and Science Fiction.* Eds. Constance Penley et al. Minneapolis: U of Minnesota P, 1991: 63-80.

Provenzo, Eugene. *Video Kids: Making Sense of Nintendo.* Cambridge, MA: Harvard UP, 1991.

Rapping, Elayne. *Media-tions: Forays into the Culture and Gender Wars.* Boston: South End, 1994.

Reichenbach, Hans. *The Direction of Time*. Berkeley: U of
   California P, 1956.

Reynolds, Richard. *Super Heroes: A Modern Mythology*. Jackson:
   University Press of Mississippi, 1992.

Roberts, Adam. *Science Fiction: the New Critical Idiom*. New
   York: Routledge, 2000.

Roberts, Robin. *A New Species: Gender and Science in Science
   Fiction*. Urbana: U of Illinois P, 1993.

---. *Sexual Generations: "Star Trek: The Next Generation" and
   Gender*. Urbana: U of Illinois P, 1999.

Robinson, Arthur H. *Early Thematic Mapping in the History of
   Cartography*. Chicago: University of Chicago Press, 1982.

Rogin, Michael Paul. *Ronald Reagan, the Movie: and Other
   Episodes in Political Demonology*. Berkeley: U of California P,
   1987.

Scarry, Elaine. *The Body in Pain: The Making and Unmaking of the
   World*. New York: Oxford UP, 1985.

Schwichtenberg, Cathy, ed. *The Madonna Connection*. Boulder,
   CO: Westview, 1993.

Scruggs, Charles. "The Two Endings of *The French Lieutenant's
   Woman*." *Modern Fiction Studies* 31.1 (1985): 95-113.

Seed, David. *American Science Fiction and the Cold War:
   Literature and Film*. Chicago: Fitzroy Dearborn, 1999.

Serres, Michel. *Genesis*. Trans. Geneviève James and James
   Nielson. Anne Arbor: U of Michigan P, 1995.

Serres, Michel. *Hermes: literature, science, philosophy*. Ed. Josué
   V. Harari & David F. Bell. Baltimore : Johns Hopkins UP,
   1982.

Shuttleworth, Sally. George Eliot and Nineteenth Century Science.
   Cambridge: Cambridge UP, 1984.

Silver, Alain and James Ursini. *The Vampire Film: From Nosferatu
   to Bram Stoker's Dracula*. New York: Limelight Editions,
   1993.

Skal, David J. *The Monster Show: A Cultural History of Horror*.
   New York: Norton, 1993.

Sobchack, Thomas and Vivian Sobchack. *An Introduction to Film.* 2nd ed. Boston: Scott, Foresman, 1987.

Sobchack, Vivian. *Screening Space: The American Science Fiction Film.* New York: Ungar, 1988.

Springer, Claudia. *Electronic Eros: Bodies and Desire in the Postindustrial Age.* Austin, TX: U of Texas P, 1996.

Stafford, Barbara Maria. *Body Criticism: Imaging the Unseen in Enlightenment Art and Medicine.* Cambridge, MA: MIT Press, 1991.

Strehle, Susan. *F`iction in the Quantum Universe.* Chapel Hill: U of North Carolina P, 1992.

Tarrat, Margaret. "Monsters from the Id." In *Film Genre: Theory and Criticism.* Ed. Barry K. Grant. Metuchen, NJ: Scarecrow Press, 1977.

Tasker, Yvonne. *Working Girls: Gender and Sexuality in Popular Cinema.* New York: Routledge, 1998.

Telotte, J.P. *Science Fiction Film.* New York: Cambridge University Press, 2001.

Telotte, J.P.. "Human Artifice and the Science Fiction Film." *Film Quarterly.* 36 (1983): 44-51.

Telotte, J.P.. *Replications: A Robotic History of the Science Fiction Film.* Urbana, IL: University of Illinois Press, 1995.

Thompson, Rosemarie Garland, ed. *Freakery: Cultural Spectacle of the Extraordinary Body.* New York: New York University Press, 1996.

Tippler, Frank J. *The Physics of Immortality: Modern Cosmology, God and the Ressurection of the Dead.* New York: Random, 1994.

Traube, Elizabeth G. *Dreaming Identities: Class, Gender, and Generation in the 1980s Hollywood Movies.* Boulder, CO: Westview, 1992.

Walker, Jeff. "The Alien: A Secret too Good to Give Away." *Rolling Stone*, 31 May 1979, 30-1.

Warburton, Eileen. "Ashes, Ashes, We all fall Down: Ourika, Cinderella, and *The French Lieutenant's Woman.*" Twentieth Century Literature 42.1 (1996): 165-186.

Warren, Robert Penn. *All the King's Men*. New York: Harcourt, 1946.

Weinstock, Jeffrey A. "Freaks in Space: 'Extraterrestrialism' and 'Deep-space Multiculturalism.'" In *Freakery: Cultural Spectacle of the Extraordinary Body*. Ed. Rosemarie Garland Thompson. New York: New York University Press, 1996.

William, Paul. *Laughing, Screaming: Modern Hollywood Horror and Comedy*. New York: Columbia University Press, 1994.

Wingrove, David, ed. *The Science Fiction Film Sourcebook*. Essex, UK: Longman, 1985.

Wolf, Mark J. P. "Abstraction in the Video Game." In *The Video Game Theory Reader*. Ed. Mark J. P. Wolf and Bernard Perron. New York: Routledge, 2003. 47-66.

Wolf, Mark J. P. and Bernard Perron eds. *The Video Game Theory Reader*. New York: Routledge, 2003.

Wood, Aylish. *Technoscience in Contemporary American Film: Beyond Science Fiction*. New York: Manchester University Press, 2002.

Wood, Robin. *Hollywood from Vietnam to Reagan*. New York: Columbia University Press, 1986.

Wurtzel, Elizabeth. *Bitch: In Praise of Difficult Women*. New York: Doubleday, 1998.

Žižek, Slavoj. *The Žižek Reader*. Ed. Elizabeth Wright and Edmond Wright. Malden, MA: Blackwell, 1999.

Hallucination, imagination, innovation: From the mind in the cave to life on the screen, increasingly virtual reality is the only human reality. *eVolve* **explains why.**

An introductory history of the "virtual body," *eVolve* explores the boundaries between a series of cultural artifacts, all of which evidence the historical moment when a technology necessary for what we now call "virtual reality" came into being in order to better understand the human fascination with, and desire for, virtuality. The discussion of simulation technologies includes visual art, cartography, narrative, drama, games and spontaneous play as simulations, miniature war games, role-playing games, computer games, virtual cinema, the internet MOOs and MUDs, massively multiplayer online communities MMOs, and, finally, artificial intelligence, the Anthropic Cosmological Principles, and Omega Point Theory. The subject matter is highly interdisciplinary and draws widely upon theoretical discussions from both the arts, humanities, and the sciences.

C. Jason Smith, Ph.D. is a former Professor of Writing and Literature for institutions such as Texas A&M University, The University of Arkansas, Louisiana State University, and The City University of New York. He now lives and writes in Richardson, Texas with his wife and two daughters, and at his family farm in Sutton, Arkansas.